AQA KS3

Activate
Know • Apply • Extend

2

Workbook: Foundation
Including Diagnostic Pinchpoint activities

Jon Clarke
Philippa Gardom Hulme
Jo Locke

Assessment Editor
Dr Andrew Chandler-Grevatt

OXFORD
UNIVERSITY PRESS

Contents

Introduction ... iv

Enquiry Processes

EP6	More on planning how to answer a question	2
EP7	More on analysing and evaluating	3
EP8	Communication	4
EP9	Evidence and sources	5
EP10	Critique claims and justify opinions	6
EP11	Risks and benefits	7
EP12	Review theories 1	8
EP13	Review theories 2	9
	Enquiry Processes Pinchpoint	10

Big Idea 1 Forces

1.3 Contact forces
1.3.1	Friction and drag	12
1.3.2	Squashing and stretching	13
1.3.3	Turning forces	14

1.4 Pressure
1.4.1	Pressure in gases	15
1.4.2	Pressure in liquids	16
1.4.3	Stress on solids	17
	Big Idea 1 Pinchpoint	18

Big Idea 2 Electromagnets

2.3 Magnetism
| 2.3.1 | Magnets and magnetic fields | 21 |

2.4 Electromagnets
2.4.1	Electromagnets	22
2.4.2	Using electromagnets	23
	Big Idea 2 Pinchpoint	24

Big Idea 3 Energy

3.3 Work
| 3.3.1 | Work, energy, and machines | 26 |

3.4 Heating and cooling
3.4.1	Energy and temperature	27
3.4.2	Energy transfer: particles	28
3.4.3	Energy transfer: radiation and insulation	29
	Big Idea 3 Pinchpoint	30

Big Idea 4 Waves

4.3 Wave effects
| 4.3.1 | Sound waves, water waves, and energy | 33 |
| 4.3.2 | Radiation and energy | 34 |

4.4 Wave properties
| 4.4.1 | Modelling waves | 35 |
| | Big Idea 4 Pinchpoint | 36 |

| | Section 1 Revision questions | 38 |
| | Section 1 Checklist | 42 |

Big Idea 5 Matter

5.3 Elements
5.3.1	Elements	43
5.3.2	Atoms	44
5.3.3	Compounds	45
5.3.4	Chemical formulae	46
5.3.5	Polymers	47

5.4 Periodic Table
5.4.1	The Periodic Table	48
5.4.2	The elements of Group 1	49
5.4.3	The elements of Group 7	50
5.4.4	The elements of Group 0	51
	Big Idea 5 Pinchpoint	52

Big Idea 6 Reactions

6.3 Types of reaction
6.3.1	Atoms in chemical reactions	55
6.3.2	Combustion	56
6.3.3	Thermal decomposition	57
6.3.4	Conservation of mass	58

6.4 Chemical energy
6.4.1	Exothermic and endothermic	59
6.4.2	Energy level diagrams	60
6.4.3	Bond energies	61
	Big Idea 6 Pinchpoint	62

Big Idea 7 Earth

7.3 Climate
7.3.1	Global warming	65
7.3.2	The carbon cycle	66
7.3.3	Climate change	67

7.4 Earth resources
7.4.1	Extracting metals	68
7.4.2	Recycling	69
	Big Idea 7 Pinchpoint	70
	Section 2 Revision questions	72
	Section 2 Checklist	75

Big Idea 8 Organisms

8.3 Breathing
8.3.1	Gas exchange	76
8.3.2	Breathing	77
8.3.3	Drugs	78
8.3.4	Alcohol	79
8.3.5	Smoking	80

8.4 Digestion
8.4.1	Nutrients	81
8.4.2	Food tests	82
8.4.3	Unhealthy diet	83
8.4.4	Digestive system	84
8.4.5	Bacteria and enzymes in digestion	85
	Big Idea 8 Pinchpoint	86

Big Idea 9 Ecosystems

9.3 Respiration
9.3.1	Aerobic respiration	89
9.3.2	Anaerobic respiration	90
9.3.3	Biotechnology	91

9.4 Photosynthesis
9.4.1	Photosynthesis	92
9.4.2	Leaves	93
9.4.3	Investigating photosynthesis	94
9.4.4	Plant minerals	95
	Big Idea 9 Pinchpoint	96

Big Idea 10 Genes

10.3 Evolution
10.3.1	Natural selection	98
10.3.2	Charles Darwin	99
10.3.3	Extinction	100
10.3.4	Preserving biodiversity	101

10.4 Inheritance
10.4.1	Inheritance	102
10.4.2	DNA	103
10.4.3	Genetics	104
10.4.4	Genetic modification	105
	Big Idea 10 Pinchpoint	106
	Section 3 Revision questions	108
	Section 3 Checklist	112

Answers 113
Periodic Table 127

Introduction

Welcome to your *Activate* 2 Workbook. This Workbook contains lots of practice questions and activities to help you to progress through the course.

Each chapter from the *Activate* 2 Student Book is covered and includes a summary of all the content you need to know. Answers to all of the questions are in the back of the Workbook so you will be able to see how well you have answered them.

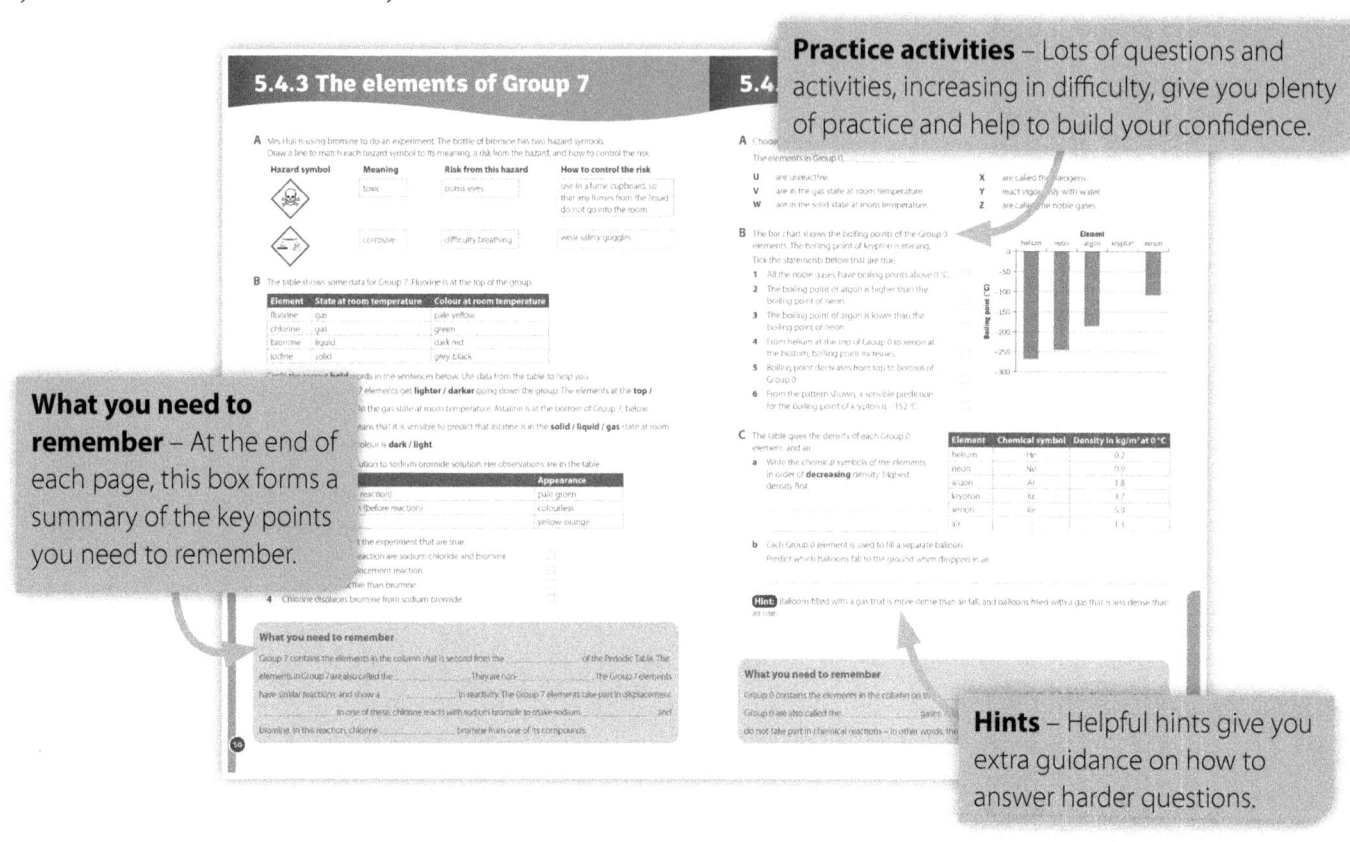

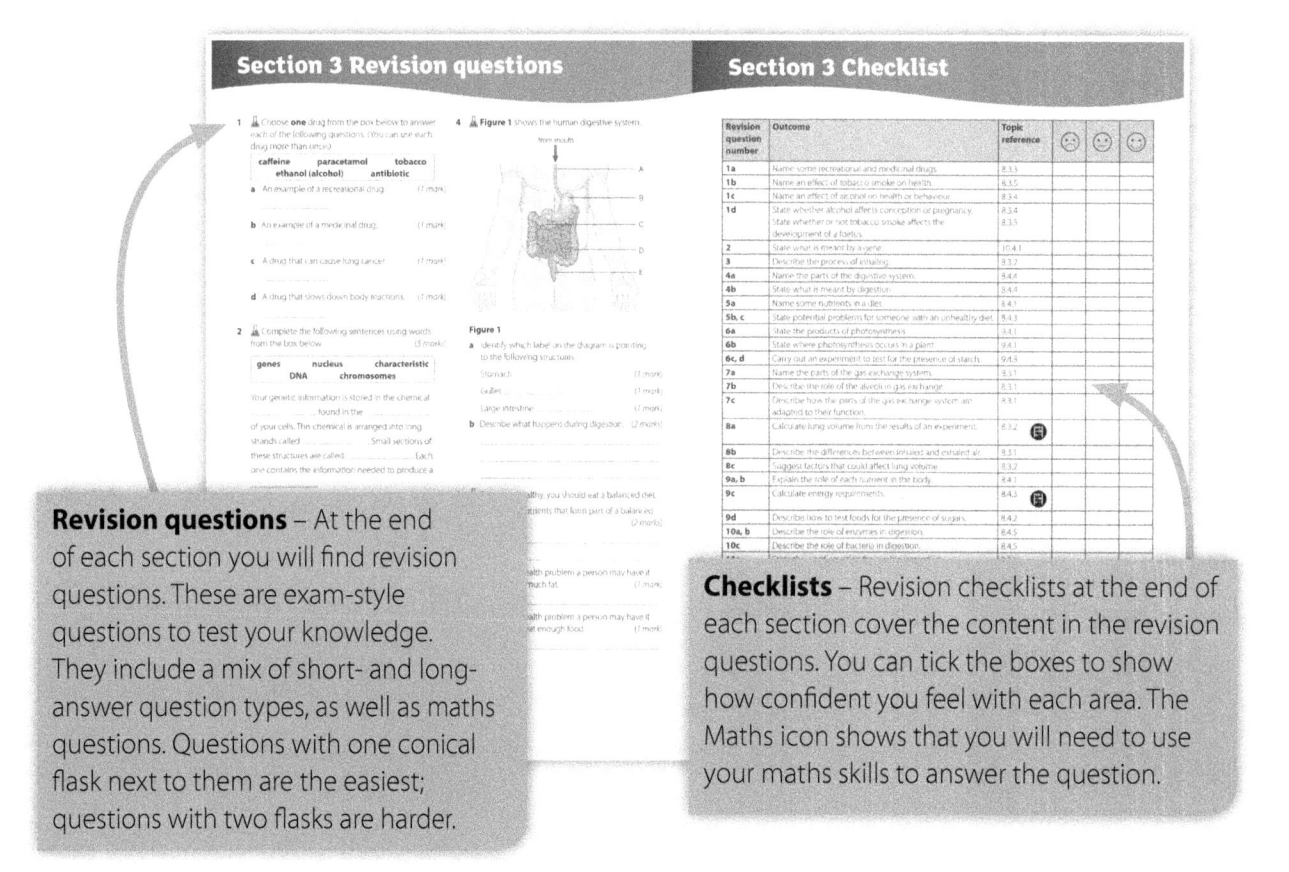

Practice activities – Lots of questions and activities, increasing in difficulty, give you plenty of practice and help to build your confidence.

What you need to remember – At the end of each page, this box forms a summary of the key points you need to remember.

Hints – Helpful hints give you extra guidance on how to answer harder questions.

Revision questions – At the end of each section you will find revision questions. These are exam-style questions to test your knowledge. They include a mix of short- and long-answer question types, as well as maths questions. Questions with one conical flask next to them are the easiest; questions with two flasks are harder.

Checklists – Revision checklists at the end of each section cover the content in the revision questions. You can tick the boxes to show how confident you feel with each area. The Maths icon shows that you will need to use your maths skills to answer the question.

Pinchpoints

A Pinchpoint is an idea or concept in science that can be challenging to learn. It is often difficult to say *why* these ideas are challenging to learn. The Pinchpoint intervention question at the end of each chapter focuses on a challenging idea from within the chapter. By answering the Pinchpoint question you will see whether you understand the concept or whether you have gone wrong. By doing the follow-up activity you will find out why you made the mistake and how to correct it.

Pinchpoint question – The Pinchpoint question is about a difficult concept from the chapter that students often get wrong. You should answer the Pinchpoint question and one follow-up activity. The Pinchpoint is multiple choice; answer the question by choosing a letter and then do the follow-up activity with the same letter.

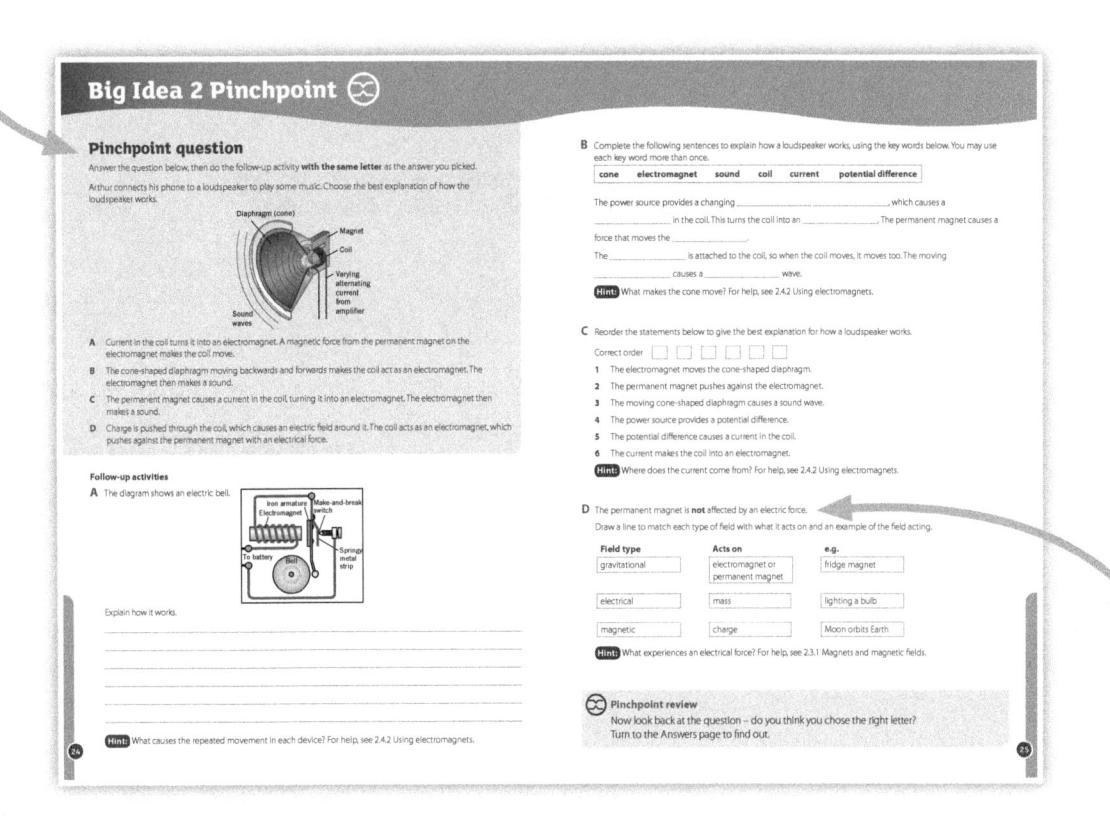

Pinchpoint follow-up – The follow-up activities will help you to better understand the difficult concept. If you got the Pinchpoint question right, the follow-up will develop your understanding further. If you got the Pinchpoint wrong, it will help you to see why you went wrong, and how to get it right next time.

EP6 More on planning how to answer a question

A Which of the following questions can be answered scientifically? Circle the number.
   1. What is the best material for making a coat?
   2. Which is the nicest flavour of fizzy drink?
   3. How does temperature affect the rate at which sugar dissolves?

B Some students wanted to investigate the effect of the steepness of a slope on the time it takes a toy car to travel down a ramp. They made a list of all the variables in their investigation.

Circle the control variables in their list.

Height of slope   **Toy car used**   **Length of slope**   **Time taken to travel down slope**

C Sort the following scientific questions into the type of scientific enquiry you should carry out
   1. How does temperature affect the rate of a chemical reaction?
   2. How are reusable bags different from each other?
   3. How do leaves on a holly bush vary?
   4. How does the number of coils around a magnet affect its strength?

Observational enquiry	Pattern-seeking enquiry

D Circle the correct **bold** words in the sentences below to explain why you should compare your results to someone else's.

If you compare your results to someone else's, and they are **similar / different**, then the experiment is **precise / repeatable**.

This means that you can have more **confidence / creativity** in your conclusion.

What you need to remember

You can investigate a question scientifically if you can collect _____. This can be in the form of observations or _____. The variable you change in an investigation is the _____ variable. The _____ variable is what you measure or observe. It is important to _____ all other variables so they don't affect the result.

You should compare the results of your investigation with others. If they are similar, the investigation is _____.

EP7 More on analysing and evaluating

A Tick the correct term for data that someone else has collected:

Primary data ☐   Additional data ☐

Secondary data ☐   Borrowed data ☐

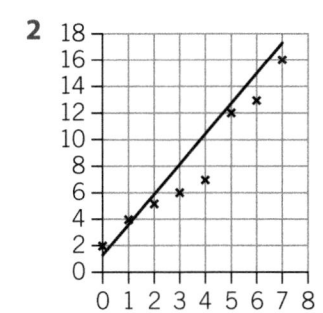

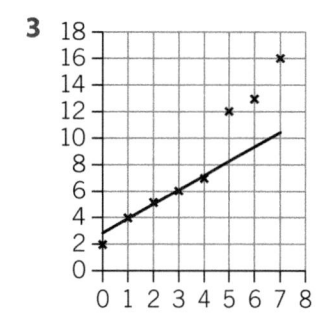

B A student made four attempts at drawing a line of best fit on their graph. Match the following sentences to the appropriate graph:

a   Line of best fit drawn too low _____

b   Line of best fit drawn too high _____

c   Line of best fit drawn incorrectly _____

d   Line of best fit drawn correctly _____

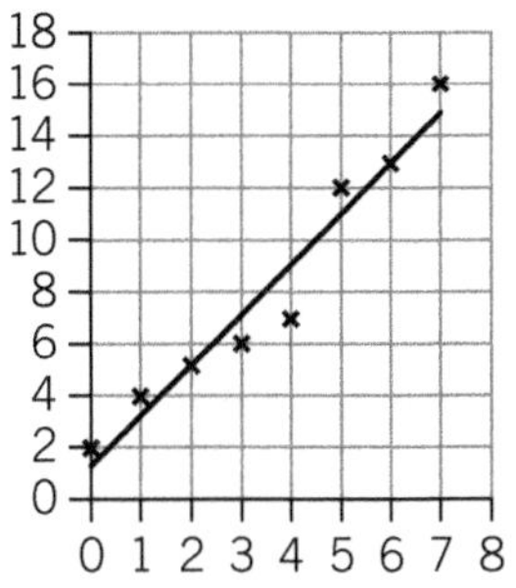

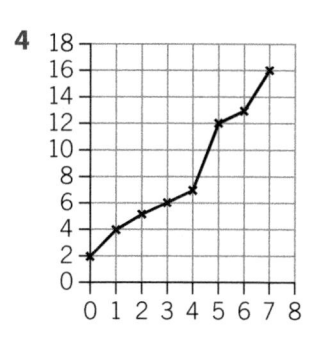

C Circle the correct bold words in the sentences below to explain what to do if your conclusion does not agree with your prediction.

If your results do not match your prediction you should:

- **repeat / stop** your investigation.
- compare with other people who carried out **a different / the same** investigation.
- look at secondary data from **the internet / a different investigation you did**.

If each of these situations shows similar results, you can be confident that your **prediction / conclusion** is correct.

What you need to remember

To identify trends on a graph you should add a line of _____. This should have approximately the _____ number of data points above and below the line.

Any data you use in an investigation that you have not collected is called _____ data. If this data matches your findings you can have more confidence in your _____.

EP8 Communication

A You work for a company that manufactures a 3D printer capable of printing edible chocolate objects. You have been asked to write part of an information leaflet to explain to buyers how the product works.

Tick the ways you can ensure your writing is suitable for this audience.

1 Use diagrams to make the use of the printer clear ☐
2 Use technical language ☐
3 Use step-by-step instructions ☐
4 Include details on the history of chocolate ☐

B Write the following paragraph again to make it more **concise**.

We measured the height of the step. The height of the step was measured using a 50 cm ruler.

_____

_____

C Draw a line to match each sample of writing with its intended purpose.

| a Today, scientists at the University of Budmouth announced that they have used a 'force field' to move matter. Like something in a science fiction film, they used beams of ultrasound to move plastic beads. | 1 Scientific journal |

| b Two ultrasound waves were superposed to produce a maximum upwards force of 12 millinewtons. The plastic beads were displaced up to a maximum of 10 mm horizontally and held to their position with a precision of 1 mm. | 2 Worksheet for primary school children |

| c Forces are pushes or pulls. You can even use invisible waves to lift something. | 3 Newspaper |

D Penny will be doing a presentation on photosynthesis to her Year 8 classmates. She has written down some information from the internet.

List four ways she could make this information better suited to her audience.

Resporation is the oxidation of sugars. plants respire too. what do they use sugar for? chloroplasts contain $C_{55}H_{72}O_5N_4Mg$ which absorbs light for photosynthesis and transfers that light to energy to power the reaction of water and carbondioxide turning into $C_6H_{12}O_6$ and oxygen and these sugars are used by the plants during resorpation and for growth.

_____

_____

What you need to remember

To make communication _____, you need to consider who will _____ it; for example, young children, the general public, or other scientists. This is called the _____. You also need to consider what the writing is intended to achieve: for example, to interest people, explain an idea, or allow scientists to carry out your experiment. This is called the _____.

EP9 Evidence and sources

A Jon is researching whether to buy a bracelet that could improve his sporting performance.

A short **video** online claims that wearing a bracelet made of a special material improves the wearer's reaction time while playing sport. It gives as evidence the experience of the wearer, who is shown playing a sport. The video was paid for by the manufacturer, although it does not say so in the video itself.

An **article** published in a peer-reviewed, scientific journal claims that wearing a bracelet made of a special material makes no significant difference to the wearer's reaction time. As evidence, they tested 100 athletes with and without the bracelet in an experiment. The article states that work was funded by the UK government.

Give **one** reason why the article is reliable and **one** reason why the video is less reliable.

_____

_____

_____

B Albie is a medical researcher, leading a team investigating a new drug. The manufacturer of the drug is paying for the research.

Madison is a journalist working for a news website that finds that it gets more readers each time it reports that a medicine causes harm.

Explain a possible cause of bias in each person's work.

Albie: _____

_____

Madison: _____

_____

C In 1989, two scientists, Fleischmann and Pons, reported some new work on the topic of 'cold fusion' directly to the media. This was two weeks before it completed peer review at a scientific journal.

Explain how peer review would have made their claims more believable.

_____

_____

What you need to remember

Scientists use _____ to help them reach conclusions. Other scientists conduct a _____ before the work is published in a _____.

An organisation that pays for scientific research is a _____. This can lead to _____.

EP10 Critique claims and justify opinions

A Draw a line to match each word to its definition.

claim	this consists of the measurements, data, or observations that support or oppose a claim
evidence	a statement that says that something is true
reasoning	ideas about what evidence means, in the form of an argument for or against a claim

B Read the news article in the box.

> **Coffee and cancer**
>
> A judge ruled in court that a substance in coffee, acrylamide, makes you more likely to get cancer. He made this decision because a scientist discovered that lab rats that drank a mixture of water and acrylamide grew cancer tumours.
>
> Another group of scientists did some different research. They asked people how much coffee they drink. After a few years, they used data from doctors to see how many of the people had cancer. There was no pattern in the results. For example, there were no more people with cancer in the group that drank the most coffee than in the group that drank the least coffee.

In the article in the box above:

a Underline the **claim** in pencil.

b Underline **evidence** that **supports** the claim in blue or black.

c Underline **evidence** that **opposes** the claim in red.

C This question is also about the news article in activity **B**.

Another scientist did experiments to find out how humans digest acrylamide, and how rats digest acrylamide. She discovered that humans and rats digest acrylamide differently.

Write down your opinion about whether or not there should be a cancer warning on takeaway coffee. Then justify your opinion using evidence from activities **B** and **C**.

Opinion _____

Evidence to justify opinion _____

_____

_____

What you need to remember

People and organisations may make a claim, which is a statement that says that something is _____.

To decide whether a claim is believable, you need to look at the scientific _____ that is offered to support or oppose a claim. Evidence can include measurements, data, and _____. You also need to use reasoning to help you to decide what the evidence means and to make an _____ for or against a claim. If you give an opinion about a claim, you must use scientific _____ to justify your opinion.

EP11 Risks and benefits

A Drones are a new invention. They are small battery-powered aircraft that do not have pilots in them. Some online companies want to use drones to deliver parcels.

In the table, tick to show which groups might benefit from drone deliveries, and which groups will not benefit.

	Group	✔ if the group might benefit from drone deliveries	✔ if the group will not benefit from drone deliveries
1	Delivery van drivers		
2	People who order clothes online		
3	Companies that sell drones		
4	People in remote hospitals who need medicines delivered quickly		
5	People who live under drone flight-paths		

B This question is also about using drones to deliver parcels.

a Suggest how delivery van drivers might be affected if online companies use drones to deliver parcels.

_____

b Suggest how using drones to deliver parcels might benefit the environment.

_____

c Suggest why some people might think it is a good idea to use drones to deliver parcels, but others might think it is a bad idea.

_____

_____

C Imagine that scientists have invented a new vaccine that stops you getting colds.

Imagine that anyone can have the vaccine, but it costs £200.

Write down two things to consider in each column of the table below.

Benefits of having the vaccine	Risks and disadvantages of having the vaccine

What you need to remember

Every discovery or invention has risks and _____. Different people are affected by a new discovery or invention in _____ ways. To make a decision, you need to weigh up the _____ and benefits of a course of action.

EP12 Review theories 1

A Draw a line to match each word to its definition.

model	a way of representing something that is too difficult to display, usually because it is too big, too small, or too complicated
theory	a statement that describes a pattern or rule about something that happens that is always true. It does not explain why something happens.
law	an explanation for patterns in observations or data that is supported by evidence

B Complete the table by writing the name of one theory in each row. Choose from the options in the box below.

| Big Bang | evolution | kinetic | combustion | germ |

Evidence	Name of theory that explains the evidence
The Universe is expanding.	
A gas spreads out to fill its container.	
When magnesium burns, the mass of magnesium oxide after burning is greater than the mass of magnesium before burning.	
Some fossils found today are of animals that are now extinct.	
If a student has a cold, many others at the same school will also catch colds.	

C Tick the statements about scientific theories that are true.
1. Most, but not all, scientific theories are supported by evidence. ☐
2. Observations and data provide evidence for scientific theories. ☐
3. Once scientists have decided on a theory, it does not change. ☐
4. The theory of combustion has changed over time. ☐
5. Observations of animals, plants, and fossils provide evidence for the theory of natural selection. ☐
6. Scientists use theories to explain observations. ☐
7. Scientists cannot use theories to make predictions. ☐
8. Scientific theories are testable. ☐

What you need to remember

A theory is an _____ for patterns in observations or data that is supported by scientific _____. For example, the behaviour of gases is explained by _____ theory. The origin of the Universe is explained by the _____ _____ theory. Scientific theories have changed over time, as scientists find new _____.

EP13 Review theories 2

A Scientific theories change over time. Tick **one** box next to each statement in the table.

	Statement	✔ This might provide a reason to change a scientific theory	✔ This increases the time for scientists to accept a new theory
a	When microscopes were invented, scientists could see smaller objects in greater detail.		
b	A scientist makes an observation that the old theory cannot explain.		
c	Scientists are familiar with the old theory.		
d	A new theory better predicts what will happen in new experiments.		
e	Religious leaders might not accept new ideas that conflict with their beliefs.		
f	Scientists collect new data that do not fit with the old theory.		

B Circle the correct **bold** words and phrases in the sentences below.

Imagine that a scientist collects new evidence that does not support an accepted theory. A new theory **does / does not** automatically exist, because someone must create it. If a scientist comes up with a new theory, they will want to convince other scientists that their theory is **correct / incorrect**. They do this by telling other scientists about their new theory. Then the scientists use logical reasoning and debate to make a decision on the new theory. This is called **contradiction / argumentation**.

C Draw a line to connect each sentence starter with the correct ending.

Scientists might test a new theory	then the new theory is stronger than it would otherwise be.
A new theory might be wrong	by trying to find out why it may be wrong.
If scientists have looked for, but not found, evidence that contradicts a new theory,	if there are observations or data that do not support it.

What you need to remember

If new evidence does not support an existing _____, a scientist may create a _____ theory to better explain the _____. The scientist will publish their ideas and discuss them at _____ to try to convince other scientists that the new theory is _____. Scientists can use a theory to make predictions, which can be _____. If the predictions are correct, more scientists will be convinced the theory is _____. The logical reasoning and debate are used to help refine a theory. This is called _____.

Enquiry Processes Pinchpoint

Pinchpoint question

Answer the question below, then do the follow-up activity **with the same letter** as the answer you picked.

When planning an investigation, it is important to identify and control some variables.

Choose the correct ending to the following sentence.

Controlling the variables is important because…

- **A** otherwise the investigation won't work.
- **B** you need to keep everything the same in investigations.
- **C** otherwise we will not know which variable made a difference.
- **D** then we will not have to repeat the experiment.

Follow-up activities

A Draw a line to match the type of variable with the definition.

Type of variable	Definition
independent variable	what you measure or observe in an investigation
dependent variable	what you change in an investigation
control variable(s)	what you keep the same in an investigation

Hint: Make sure you know the difference between these key words. For help, see EP6 More on planning how to answer a question, and the Glossary.

B A student investigates the link between the thickness of a piece of elastic and its length when stretched.

Identify each of the variables below as independent, dependent, or control.

Variable	Variable type
Thickness of elastic	
Temperature of elastic	
Material the elastic is made of	
Length of elastic	
Mass used the stretch the elastic	

Hint: Remember that the variable you are observing or measuring (the reason you are doing your experiment) is called the dependent variable. You need to learn the three types of variable. For help, see EP6 More on planning how to answer a question, and the Glossary.

C Sometimes we cannot control all variables. A student compares the organisms living in a polluted pond with those living in a clean pond.

List the variables in the environment that cannot be controlled.

_____

_____

Hint: The ponds will be outside, in different places. What could be different? For help, see EP6 More on planning how to answer a question.

D A student investigates how much copper sulfate can be dissolved at different temperatures.

Identify which actions control variables during the experiment.

	Actions	Control ✓
1	Use the same volume of water at each temperature	
2	Increase the range of readings, e.g. 10 °C to 100 °C	
3	Get a different person to do the experiment	
4	Use the same mass of copper sulfate at each temperature	
5	Take more readings, e.g. 5 readings instead of 3	
6	Use the same size and volume of beaker	
7	Stir each beaker the same number of times	

Hint: Focus on controlling the variables you are not measuring. For help, see EP6 More on planning how to answer a question.

Pinchpoint review

Now look back at the question – do you think you chose the right letter?
Turn to the Answers page to find out.

1.3.1 Friction and drag

A Draw a line to match each force with its cause and an example.

Force	Cause	Example
water resistance	rough surfaces are touching	a dolphin swimming
air resistance	must push many liquid particles out of the way	brakes on a bus
friction	must push many gas particles out of the way	a bird flying

B Complete the table to describe the role of friction or drag forces in each situation.

Situation	Role of friction or drag forces
A boat when its engine stops.	
A mechanic putting oil on a bicycle chain.	
Walking forwards on a pavement.	
A skydiver opening her parachute.	

C a A leaf falls from a tree. Initially it is moving very slowly and only one force is acting on the leaf. Suggest which force this is.

_____

b As the leaf falls, it speeds up and another force acts on it, getting larger as it speeds up. Suggest which other force is acting.

_____

c After a while, the two forces are equal and acting in opposite directions so that there is no resultant force. Predict what will happen to the speed and direction of the leaf while it is still in the air.

_____

What you need to remember

_____ grips objects because, although their surfaces might look smooth, they are actually _____. One way to reduce friction is to use _____. Drag forces, such as _____ resistance or _____ resistance, happen because an object has to push air or water molecules out of the way. Making an object more _____ is a way to reduce drag. If no other force is applied, friction and drag forces cause an object to _____ _____ or stop. Drag and friction are examples of _____ forces, where the object affected must be touching the substance causing the force.

The total of all the forces acting on an object is called the _____ force. If this is zero then the object is in _____ – if it was stationary then it will stay _____, or if it was moving it will keep moving with the _____ speed and _____.

The unit of force is the _____, symbol N.

1.3.2 Squashing and stretching

A Complete these sentences about the effects of forces on objects. You can choose from the following words:

| supports   stretch   deforms   compress |

When a falling ball hits the floor, the ball _____. Forces can

_____ (squash) or _____ objects.

B The statements below can be reordered to explain how solid surfaces provide a support force. Read the statements and write down the order of statements that you think will give the best explanation.

Correct order ☐ ☐ ☐ ☐

1. Your weight pushes the particles in the floor together.
2. The Earth pulls down on you with a force of gravity, your weight.
3. The bonds push back and support you.
4. The bonds between the particles in the floor are compressed.

C A spring obeys Hooke's Law. It stretches by 5 cm when a force of 20 N is applied to it.

Predict how far it will stretch if a force of 40 N is applied to it. _____ cm

D a On the graph paper on page 20, plot a graph of extension (y-axis) against force (x-axis) using the data in the table. Label the axes, and draw a line of best fit.

b Does the graph you have drawn obey Hooke's Law?
Circle your answer.   **Yes / No**

c Give a reason for your answer: _____

_____

_____

Force (N)	Extension (cm)
1.0	0.5
2.0	1.0
3.0	1.4
4.0	1.8
5.0	2.3
6.0	2.9
7.0	3.3
8.0	3.7

What you need to remember

Forces can change the shape of objects, or _____ them. Forces can _____ (squash) or stretch objects. When you stand on the floor, your weight compresses the bonds between the particles in the floor. They push back and the floor _____ up on you when you stand on it. This support force from the floor is called the _____ force. Bungee cords, springs, and even lift cables all _____ when you exert a force on them. The amount that they stretch is called the _____. A bungee cord will pull back on the person with a force called _____. Springs are special: if you double the force on a spring, the extension will _____. This relationship is called _____ and it is a _____ relationship. Beyond a particular force, the spring will not go back to its original length when you remove the force. This is the _____ limit.

Any graph that shows a straight line means there is a _____ relationship between the variables. A proportional relationship is a special kind of _____ relationship because the straight line goes through the _____ of the graph.

13

1.3.3 Turning forces

A The photograph shows a ruler balanced with two apples.
This situation obeys the law of moments.
Give the law of moments using these keywords.

| equilibrium | sum | clockwise |
| anticlockwise | moments |

_____

_____

B Moment of force can be calculated by the formula:
moment (N m) = force (N) × perpendicular distance from the pivot (m)

  a Callum applies 5.0 N of force to a door handle 0.50 m from the hinges to open the door.
Calculate the moment of force.

_____

  b Molly holds a 50 N bag of groceries. Her forearm is 0.40 m from her elbow to her hand.
Calculate the moment of force of the groceries about her elbow.

_____

  c Tightrope walkers must keep their centre of gravity directly above the rope.
Explain why this is important.

_____

_____

_____

What you need to remember

When we apply a force to a door that can _____ on its hinges, there is a turning effect called a _____. The _____ of a force is defined and calculated as the _____ applied (N) times the perpendicular _____ to the _____ (m). It has the unit _____ _____, symbol (N m). If a _____ of one newton is applied one metre from a _____, then there is a _____ of one N m. If the sum of the moments in a clockwise direction are equal to the sum of the moments in the anticlockwise direction, the object is in _____ and it will not start turning. This is the _____ _____. The centre of gravity (centre of mass) is the point through which the _____ appears to act. If the centre of gravity of an object is directly _____ or _____ the pivot there will be _____ moment making it turn. If it is to the side of the pivot, the object will start to _____ due to the moment.

1.4.1 Pressure in gases

A When you pump up a tyre with a bicycle pump you change the pressure of the air in the pump.

   a Sketch the arrangement of air particles in the bike pump after being compressed.

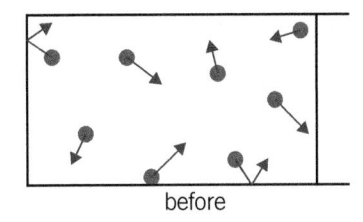

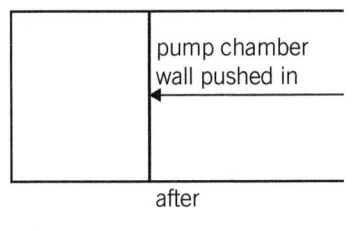

   b Explain why the cylinder of a bike pump must be made of a strong, rigid material.

_____

B **a** Draw a line to match each factor with its effect on pressure and the reason.

| An increase in **temperature** | causes an **increase** in pressure | because the particles have **further** to travel so collide **less** often. |
| An increase in **volume** | causes a **decrease** in pressure | because the gas particles move **faster**, so collide **harder** and **more** often. |

   b A gas exerts a force of 24 N over an area of 1.5 m². The formula for calculating pressure is: pressure (N/m²) = $\frac{\text{force (N)}}{\text{area (m}^2\text{)}}$.

Calculate the pressure of the gas.

_____

C The photograph shows a pilot dressed to cope with the effects of being at high altitude.

Describe how atmospheric pressure changes with height and **one** effect this has on people.

_____
_____
_____

What you need to remember

A substance without a fixed shape, such as a gas or liquid, is called a _____. Gases, such as air, exert _____ because of collisions between the gas _____, and between them and any surface they touch. When we squeeze a gas it is _____, which increases its pressure and its _____.

Pressure is defined and calculated as the _____ applied (N) divided by the _____ over which it is applied (m²). It has the unit _____, symbol N/m². If a _____ of one newton is applied over one square metre, there is a _____ of 1 N/m².

The air around us is at _____, which causes a force pushing in on our skin. This is balanced by the pressure from inside our bodies. As you go higher, such as up a mountain, _____ gets _____.

1.4.2 Pressure in liquids

A a For each object, circle whether you expect it to float or sink when placed in water.

boat: **sink** **float**
pebble: **sink** **float**
basketball: **sink** **float**

b Describe why some objects float and others sink.

Float _____

Sink _____

B a Describe how liquid pressure changes with depth as a submersible probe sinks deeper in the ocean.

_____

_____

b The submersible has a surface area of 2.4 m² and the ocean exerts a force on it of 750 000 N. The formula for calculating pressure is: pressure (N/m²) = $\frac{\text{force (N)}}{\text{area (m}^2\text{)}}$.

Calculate the water pressure at the surface.

C Complete each diagram to show the forces on each object.

a A boat floating.

b An anchor about to sink.

What you need to remember

Liquids, such as water, exert _____ because of how the particles push against each other and anything they touch. There is a difference in _____ between the top and bottom of an object which is in water. This causes a force called _____. This is what causes people to float when they are swimming. When liquids are squeezed their _____ hardly changes at all: they are

_____.

1.4.3 Stress on solids

A Stress can be calculated by the formula:

$$\text{stress (N/m}^2\text{)} = \frac{\text{force (N)}}{\text{surface area (m}^2\text{)}}$$

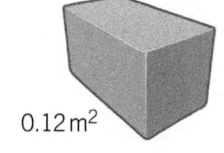

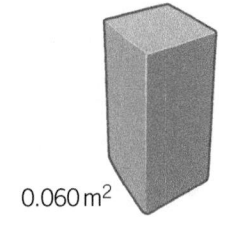

a The diagram shows a child's foam block lying flat and standing on its end. The block weighs 20 N.
Calculate the stress on each face of the block.

0.12 m²   0.060 m²

Lying flat: _____

On its end: _____

b Three blocks are stacked on top of each other, lying flat.
Calculate how much stress is on the floor under the bottom block.

_____

B a A box of cereal has a weight of 5.0 N, and an area of 0.010 m².
Calculate the stress it exerts on its kitchen shelf.

_____

b A garden shed and its foundations have a weight of 2500 N, and an area of 6.4 m².
Calculate the stress it exerts on the ground.

_____

C Some historic homes have floors made of wood that need to be protected from damage.
Use the idea of stress to explain why narrow 'stiletto' heels might damage the floor, but the same person wearing shoes with a wider heel is unlikely to.

_____
_____
_____

What you need to remember

_____ is defined and calculated as the _____ applied (N) divided by the _____ over which it is applied (m²). It has the unit _____, symbol N/m². If a _____ of one newton is applied over one square metre, there is a _____ of 1 N/m². A _____ force exerted on a _____ area exerts a large _____ on the surface, whereas the same force spread over a _____ area will result in _____ stress on the surface.

Big Idea 1 Pinchpoint

Pinchpoint question

Answer the question below, then do the follow-up activity **with the same letter** as the answer you picked.

Esme has squashed an empty plastic drinks bottle, reducing the volume inside it. The bottle contains only air and has the lid tightly screwed shut.

Select the statement that best describes what has happened to the pressure of the air inside the bottle.

A   There has been no change in temperature, so there is no change in pressure.

B   The gas particles collide with each other and the inside of the container more often, so pressure is higher.

C   The bottle has a smaller surface area, so the pressure is lower.

D   The smaller volume means that there are fewer gas particles to collide, so they collide less often and pressure is lower.

Follow-up activities

A   Gas pressure is caused by collisions between the gas particles and the container walls.

Imagine two plastic drinks bottles, X and Y, with the same volume and at the same temperature, but one contains twice as many gas particles.

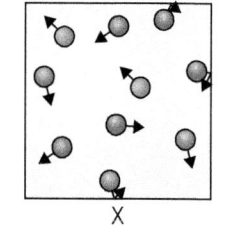

   a   Compare the number of collisions in the two bottles.

   _____

   _____

   b   Compare the pressure in two bottles.

   _____

   Hint: What is the relationship between density and pressure? For help, see 1.4.1 Pressure in gases.

B   a   When pumping up a bike tyre, the cyclist pushes a piston down to compress the air, which then goes into the tyre. Explain in terms of the gas particles and pressure why the air moves into the tyre.

   _____

   _____

   _____

   _____

   b   If you pull back the plunger on a syringe, air will flow into it. Explain in terms of the gas particles and pressure why this happens.

   _____

   _____

   _____

   _____

   Hint: What is the relationship between density and pressure? For help, see 1.4.1 Pressure in gases.

18

C a Recall the formula relating fluid pressure and area.

_____

b Calculate the pressure if a force of 10 N is applied over an area of 2.4 m².

_____

c Calculate the pressure if the same force is applied over an area of 1.2 m².

_____

d Describe the relationship between area and pressure.

_____
_____

Hint: What area causes a large pressure? For help, see 1.4.1 Pressure in gases.

D The drinks bottle has air trapped inside, so the amount of gas is constant.

a Circle what happens to density if the same amount of gas is squeezed into a smaller volume.

increases / remains the same / decreases

b Describe the relationship between density and pressure, for a fixed amount of gas.

_____
_____

c Describe the relationship between volume and pressure, for a fixed amount of gas.

_____
_____

d Describe what happened to the pressure when the air tank was dented.

_____
_____

Hint: What is density? For help, see 1.4.1 Pressure in gases.

Pinchpoint review

Now look back at the question – do you think you chose the right letter?
Turn to the Answers page to find out.

This is a repeat of activity D from 1.3.2 Squashing and stretching. Draw your graph here and then answer the questions on page 13.

D On the graph paper below, plot a graph of extension (*y*-axis) against force (*x*-axis) using the data in the table. Label the axes, and draw a line of best fit.

Force (N)	Extension (cm)
1.0	0.5
2.0	1.0
3.0	1.4
4.0	1.8
5.0	2.3
6.0	2.9
7.0	3.3
8.0	3.7

2.3.1 Magnets and magnetic fields

A a Complete this diagram to show the magnetic field lines around a bar magnet.

| N | S |

b Complete this diagram to show the magnetic field lines around a bar magnet that is **stronger** than in part **a**.

| N | S |

B For each combination of magnets below, write whether they will attract, repel, or have no effect.

a | N | | S | _____
b | S | | N | _____
c | N | | N | _____
d | S | | S | _____

C Complete the diagram to show the Earth's magnetic field.

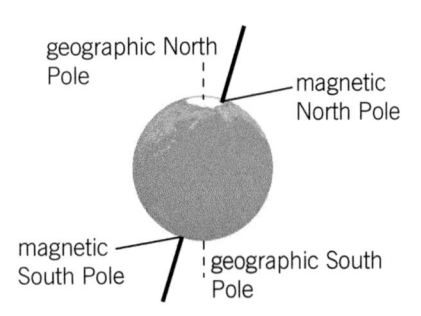

geographic North Pole
magnetic North Pole
magnetic South Pole
geographic South Pole

What you need to remember

Some materials are attracted to a magnet, or can be themselves turned into permanent _____.
These are called _____ _____, and include the elements _____, nickel, and cobalt, and some types of steel, which contains _____. Every magnet has a _____ _____ and a _____. A compass is a magnet that is free to rotate.
It will spin until its _____ pole points to the _____ magnetic North Pole, which is actually a magnetic _____ pole.
Two magnets will attract each other if they have _____ poles nearest to each other, or repel if they have the _____ poles nearest to each other. We say that magnets are surrounded by a _____, which we can detect using a compass or iron filings. We can represent this by drawing _____, which point from the north pole to the south pole, and show where a field is strong by drawing _____ of them. The field causes a magnetic _____.

2.4.1 Electromagnets

A **a** Give **one** difference between permanent magnets and electromagnets.

_____

b Sketch an electromagnet and label its main features.

B Describe **two** ways to make an electromagnet stronger.

_____

_____

C **a** Draw a line to join each type of field to the item that can cause it.

electric field		current in a wire
magnetic field		charge
gravitational field		mass

b Describe how the magnetic field strength of the electromagnet wire (current-carrying wire) varies as distance from the wire increases.

_____

D A group of students wants to investigate the effect current has on the strength of an electromagnet. They are provided with an electromagnet, an iron rod, a variable power supply, an ammeter and many steel paper clips.

Describe how they should carry out the experiment, including how they should use the equipment and what results they should collect.

_____

_____

_____

What you need to remember

An electromagnet consists of a _____ of wire with many _____, wrapped around a _____. To make an electromagnet stronger, create _____ on the coil, use a larger _____, or use a _____ in the core that is easy to _____, such as iron. Electromagnets can be more useful than _____ magnets because they can be _____ _____ or made far stronger. The magnetic _____ around an electromagnet is very similar to that around a _____ magnet. Another name for a coil is a _____.

22

2.4.2 Using electromagnets

A When you ring a doorbell, you are using electromagnetism. Use the terms below to label the diagram of an electric bell.

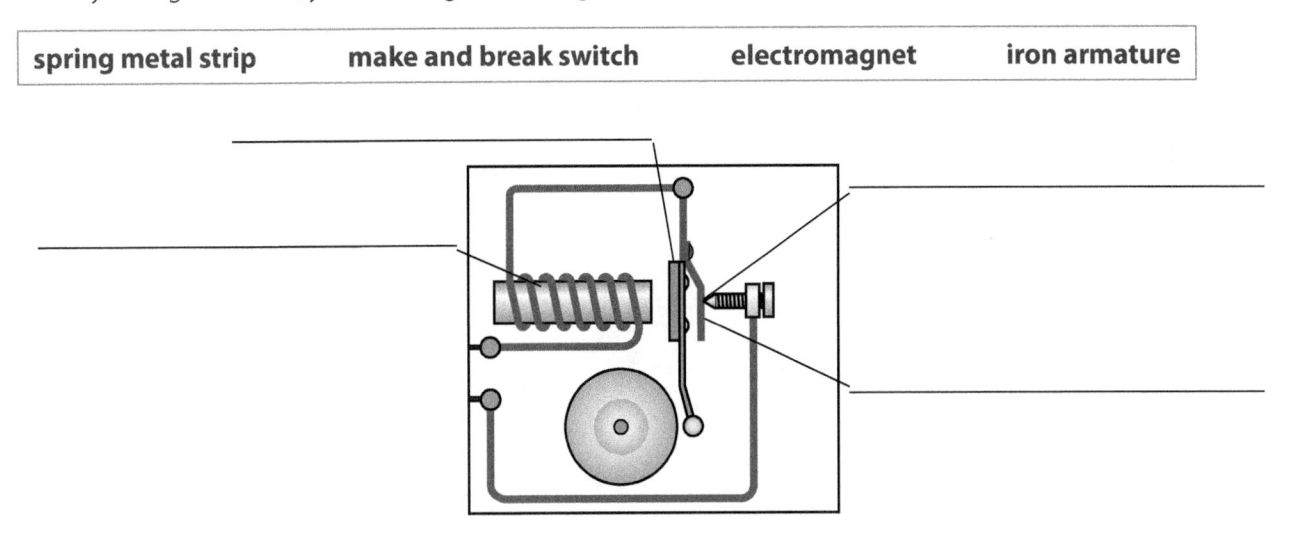

| spring metal strip | make and break switch | electromagnet | iron armature |

B Reorder the statements below to describe how a loudspeaker works.

Correct order ☐ ☐ ☐ ☐

1. Current flows in coil.
2. Connect coil to the power source.
3. Coil becomes an electromagnet.
4. Forces between the coil and the permanent magnet make the cone move.

C Describe one use of an electromagnet other than a bell, loudspeaker, or circuit breaker.

_____

D Use the diagram to help you explain how a circuit breaker helps to keep you safe in case of a dangerously high current.

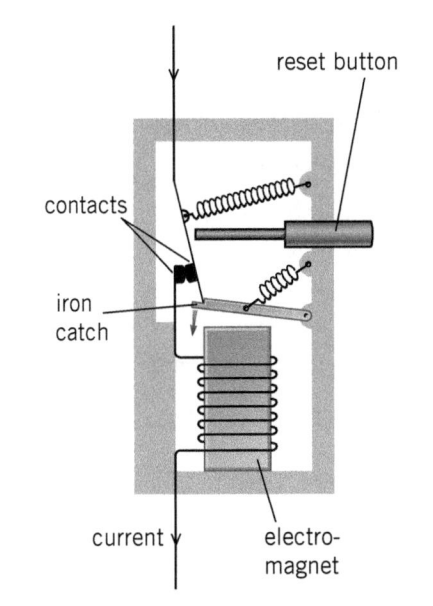

_____

_____

_____

What you need to remember

In an electric bell, when a switch is closed, _____ passes through a _____, making an electromagnet. The coil attracts an _____ armature, which then breaks the circuit. The repeated making and breaking of the circuit rings the _____.

A circuit breaker has an _____ armature completing the circuit, which is held in place with springs. When the _____ in a nearby _____ becomes too large, the magnetic field created attracts the armature out of place and breaks the circuit. It is designed to protect the devices from power surges and to protect people from electric shocks.

A loudspeaker depends on a varying _____ in a coil causing a varying magnetic field which attracts and repels a permanent _____, moving the cone of the loudspeaker in and out.

Big Idea 2 Pinchpoint

Pinchpoint question

Answer the question below, then do the follow-up activity **with the same letter** as the answer you picked.

Arthur connects his phone to a loudspeaker to play some music. Choose the best explanation of how the loudspeaker works.

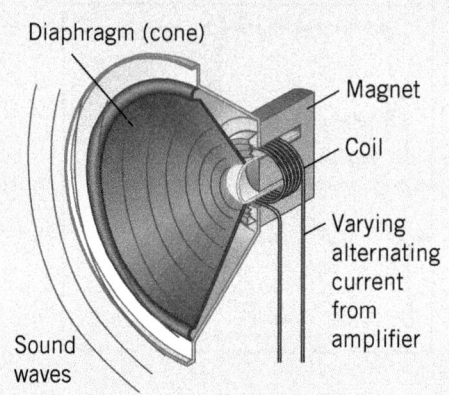

A Current in the coil turns it into an electromagnet. A magnetic force from the permanent magnet on the electromagnet makes the coil move.

B The cone-shaped diaphragm moving backwards and forwards makes the coil act as an electromagnet. The electromagnet then makes a sound.

C The permanent magnet causes a current in the coil, turning it into an electromagnet. The electromagnet then makes a sound.

D Charge is pushed through the coil, which causes an electric field around it. The coil acts as an electromagnet, which pushes against the permanent magnet with an electrical force.

Follow-up activities

A The diagram shows an electric bell.

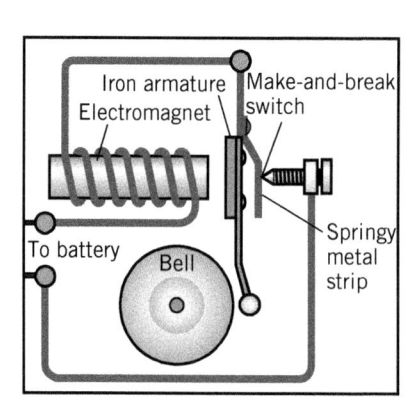

Explain how it works.

_____
_____
_____
_____
_____

Hint: What causes the repeated movement in each device? For help, see 2.4.2 Using electromagnets.

B Complete the following sentences to explain how a loudspeaker works, using the key words below. You may use each key word more than once.

| cone | electromagnet | sound | coil | current | potential difference |

The power source provides a changing _____ _____, which causes a _____ in the coil. This turns the coil into an _____. The permanent magnet causes a force that moves the _____.

The _____ is attached to the coil, so when the coil moves, it moves too. The moving _____ causes a _____ wave.

Hint: What makes the cone move? For help, see 2.4.2 Using electromagnets.

C Reorder the statements below to give the best explanation for how a loudspeaker works.

Correct order ☐ ☐ ☐ ☐ ☐ ☐

1 The electromagnet moves the cone-shaped diaphragm.
2 The permanent magnet pushes against the electromagnet.
3 The moving cone-shaped diaphragm causes a sound wave.
4 The power source provides a potential difference.
5 The potential difference causes a current in the coil.
6 The current makes the coil into an electromagnet.

Hint: Where does the current come from? For help, see 2.4.2 Using electromagnets.

D The permanent magnet is **not** affected by an electric force.

Draw a line to match each type of field with what it acts on and an example of the field acting.

Field type	Acts on	e.g.
gravitational	electromagnet or permanent magnet	fridge magnet
electrical	mass	lighting a bulb
magnetic	charge	Moon orbits Earth

Hint: What experiences an electrical force? For help, see 2.3.1 Magnets and magnetic fields.

Pinchpoint review

Now look back at the question – do you think you chose the right letter?
Turn to the Answers page to find out.

3.3.1 Work, energy, and machines

A Simple machines include devices like levers. Fill in the gaps to complete these sentences about levers. You may use a word more than once.

| greater | multiplier | lever | conserves | smaller |

Most people use a _____ to open a tin of paint. This is because you can use a much _____ force. The force applied to the lid is _____ than the force that you apply with your hand. A lever is a force _____. The input force is _____ than the output force.

A lever _____ energy.

B Work done can be calculated using the formula:

work done (J) = force (N) × distance travelled in direction of force (m)

An office worker has a weight of 750 N. He climbs the stairs 20 m vertically to his desk. Calculate the work done.

C a A mechanic applies a force of 120 N to a lever to lift a car, moving the lever through a distance of 0.40 m. Calculate the work he does on the lever.

b The mechanic has done work on the lever. To lift the car, the lever must do work on the car. Suggest the maximum work that the lever can do on the car and give a reason.

What you need to remember

When an object is moved by a force through a distance, for instance if we deform a spring, we say that _____ is done. The distance moved in a straight line from its starting point is also called its _____. It is a way of transferring _____, like heating. Work _____ is defined and calculated as the force (N) times the distance moved in direction of force (m). It has the same unit as energy, the _____, symbol J. If a _____ of one newton moves an object one metre, then one joule of _____ is done, and one joule of _____ is transferred between stores. Some devices can reduce the force you need to apply to move an object, so that the output force is _____ than the input force. Other devices can increase the distance the object moves when you apply a force. All such devices are called _____. Examples include _____, pulleys, and _____.

3.4.1 Energy and temperature

A When an object is heated, both its temperature and the energy in its thermal energy store increase. Fill in the gaps to complete the sentences below about temperature and energy.

| increases | J | °C | move / vibrate | thermal | increases | stays the same |

Temperature is measured in _____. As the mass of an object changes, its temperature _____. As we increase the mass of an object, for example by adding more water to a glass, its temperature _____.

Energy is measured in _____. As the mass of the object increases, the amount of energy in its _____ store _____.

B a Ice is composed of water particles. Describe what happens to them when you heat it.
_____

b Describe what happens to the particles in liquid water when you heat it.
_____

C a Katie places a bowl of hot soup on the table in the kitchen. Describe what happens to the temperatures of the soup and the air in the room.
_____
_____

b Katie places the cold, empty bowl in warm water in the sink. The temperatures of the bowl and water will change until they reach equilibrium.
Explain what is meant by equilibrium.
_____
_____

What you need to remember

We describe how hot or cold something is as its _____. We measure this using a _____, using the unit of _____, symbol _____.
If a hotter object is put in contact with a colder one, the hot one will heat the cold one until they reach the _____ temperature and are in _____, that is until _____ energy is transferred between their _____ energy stores.

The energy that you need to raise the temperature of a material depends on the _____ of material and the _____ of material, as well as on how much you want to raise the temperature.

3.4.2 Energy transfer: particles

A Circle the correct keywords to complete these sentences.

A thermal insulator can **increase / reduce** heat loss compared to conductors. Energy is transferred much **slower / faster** through an insulator. Gases are good **insulators / conductors** because their particles are far apart.

B a The photograph shows an example of thermal conduction.
Explain how energy is transferred during conduction.

_____

_____

b The photograph shows an example of convection.
Explain how energy is transferred during convection.

_____

_____

C The diagram shows an experiment to measure which materials are the best thermal conductors.

A timer is started when the ends of the rods are heated and stopped when the wax at the other end melts. The table shows the results for three materials.

Rod	Material	Time taken (s)
A	glass	More than 1000
B	aluminium	80
C	copper	48

Write a conclusion, including which material is the best conductor.

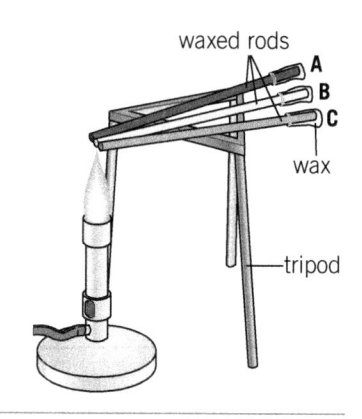

_____

_____

_____

_____

What you need to remember

Energy can be transferred by heating – this transfers the energy from a _____ energy store associated with a _____ object into the thermal store of a _____ object. This can happen in three ways. Particles in a hot material _____. When they collide with their neighbours, making them vibrate, we call that thermal _____. This process happens fastest with materials in a _____ state and slowest with materials in a _____ state. Materials where this happens very slowly are called thermal _____.

When you heat a liquid or gas, its particles move further apart so the fluid becomes less _____. The hotter, less _____ fluid then rises, moving to a place that is colder. The colder, denser fluid then _____ and the process is repeated. This process is called _____. The movement of the fluid from one place to another is called a _____ _____.

3.4.3 Energy transfer: radiation and insulation

A a Explain why black laundry dries more quickly than white clothes when hung outside on a sunny day.
_____
_____

b Water can be heated by the Sun using the device shown. The water gets hottest when matt black paint is used in the device, rather than shiny black or any other colour or finish. Explain why.
_____
_____

B a Draw a line to connect each method of energy transfer to its cause.

Conduction	Emission and absorption of infrared
Convection	Particles moving from a hotter place to a colder place
Radiation	In solids, particles vibrating and colliding with neighbours

b Explain how energy is transferred by radiation using these keywords:

| radiation | emit | absorb | infrared | hot objects | heating |

_____
_____
_____

C Describe how the following slow down thermal energy transfer.

a i Plastic handle on a kettle. _____

ii Foam between the walls of your house. _____

iii Foil blanket wrapped around a runner at the end of a race. _____

b For each of the examples above, identify the type of energy transfer from the list below.

| radiation | convection | conduction |

i _____   ii _____   iii _____

What you need to remember

To transfer thermal energy by _____ or _____ requires particles. However, these are not needed for heating by _____. Hot objects emit _____, sometimes known as thermal radiation or heat. This can be detected using a _____ _____, for instance to help firefighters find people in a smoke-filled room. When objects _____ this radiation, they warm up. It is a wave like light and can be _____, _____, or _____. Surfaces that have a _____ colour and _____ finish absorb infrared better than ones that are _____ and _____.

Big Idea 3 Pinchpoint

Pinchpoint question

Answer the question below, then do the follow-up activity **with the same letter** as the answer you picked.

Anna is studying thermal insulation to help keep people's homes warm. She is looking at the processes that cool the inside of a home. Choose the best explanation below.

A   A particle of the solid wall **moves** from the **cold** air outside the building to the warmer inside of the room, carrying thermal energy with it. This is called **conduction**.

B   A particle of the solid wall makes its neighbours **vibrate**, transferring some thermal energy to them. This is called **conduction**.

C   A particle of the solid wall **moves** from the **hot** inside to the cold outside, carrying thermal energy with it. This is called **convection**.

D   A particle of the solid wall makes its neighbours **vibrate**, transferring some thermal energy to them. This is called **convection**.

Follow-up activities

A Conduction transfers energy from hotter things to colder things, as shown in the diagram.

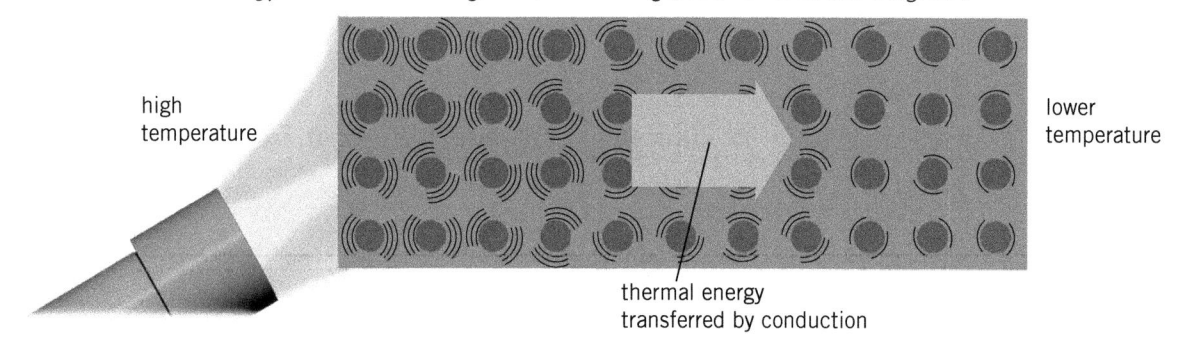

high temperature

lower temperature

thermal energy transferred by conduction

Fill in the gaps to explain the process using these key words.

| conduction | vibrating | forces | gases | liquids |
| vibrate | vibrate | pushes | rise | kinetic |

When a solid is heated, its particles _____ in place, without the particle moving to a new position as happens in _____ and _____. In a solid, particles experience _____ from their neighbours. When one particle starts _____ more, it _____ on its neighbours, making them _____ more. This increases their _____ energy store and causes the temperature to _____. In this way, energy is transferred from a warmer place in the solid to a colder place by _____.

Hint: How does conduction occur? For help, see 3.4.2 Energy transfer: particles.

B Some materials are good thermal insulators. For each material shown below, identify whether it is a good or a poor thermal insulator and explain why.

a Metals _____

_____

b Most plastics _____

_____

c Fleece _____

_____

Hint: What makes a good thermal insulator? For help, see 3.4.2 Energy transfer: particles.

C Convection involves particles moving from one position to another in the material. The diagram shows the arrangement of particles in solids, liquids, and gases.

solid   liquid

gas

Describe how the particles can move in each state and therefore which can pass on energy by convection.

Solid _____

_____

Liquid _____

_____

Gas _____

_____

Hint: How do particles move in each state of matter? For help, see 3.4.1 Energy and temperature.

31

D Identify each diagram as radiation, conduction, or convection, and give a brief description of how the thermal energy is transferred in each process.

Diagram	Energy transfer method	Description
thermal store at a high temperature — thermal store at a low temperature		
(saucepan on stove)		
(fire)		

Hint: Which ways is energy transferred? For help, see 3.4.2 Energy transfer: particles and 3.4.3 Energy transfer: radiation and insulation.

Pinchpoint review

Now look back at the question – do you think you chose the right letter?
Turn to the Answers page to find out.

4.3.1 Sound waves, water waves, and energy

A **a** Label the diagram of the microphone using these key words:

diaphragm   magnet
coil   sound waves

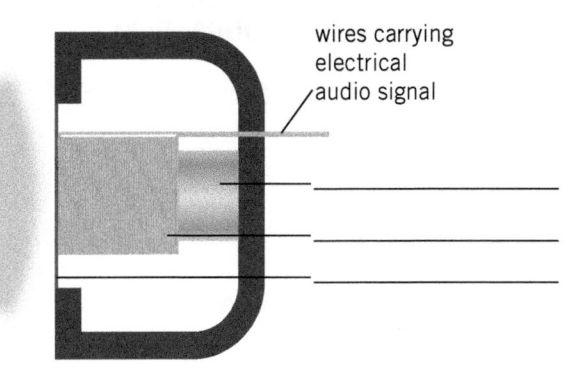

b Label the diagram of the loudspeaker using these key words:

magnet   diaphragm (cone)
sound waves   coil

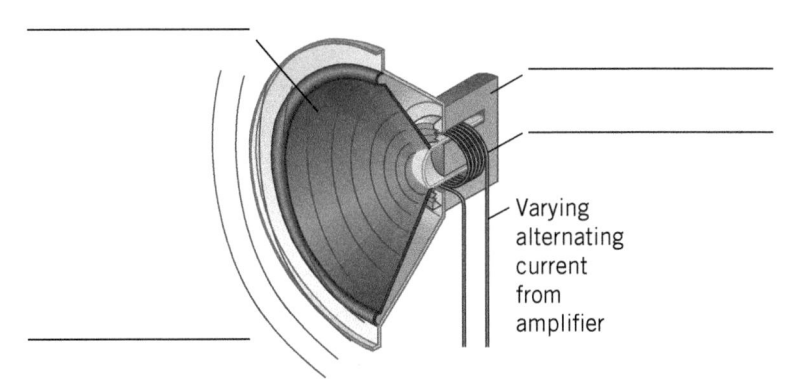

c Draw a line to connect each device with how it relates to sound waves, electrical signals, potential difference, and pressure.

Microphone	Input is an electrical signal	Output is an electrical signal	Turns varying potential difference into a changing pressure
Loudspeaker	Absorbs sound waves	Emits sound waves	Turns changing pressure into a varying potential difference

B Circle the correct answer to describe how the properties of sound waves relate to the energy that they transfer.

a If a wave has a bigger amplitude, it transfers **less / the same / more** energy.

b If a wave has a higher frequency, it transfers **less / the same / more** energy.

C Using the key words below, describe how a microphone detects sound and converts it into an electrical signal.

diaphragm   sound wave   vibrate   coil   potential difference

_____

_____

What you need to remember

In a sound wave, there are places where air particles are squeezed closer together, called _____, and other places where they are further apart, called _____. Therefore, sound is a _____ wave. A device that converts a sound wave into an electrical signal is called a _____. A device that converts an electrical signal into a sound wave is a _____. A sound which has a frequency higher than humans can hear, above _____ Hz, is called _____.

4.3.2 Radiation and energy

A Arrange these parts of the electromagnetic spectrum in order, starting with the largest wavelength.

| ultraviolet | visible light | X-rays | microwaves |
| gamma rays | radio waves | infrared |

B a Name **two** wave bands of the electromagnetic spectrum that cannot be seen with the naked eye and give a use for each.

Band 1 _____ Use _____

Band 2 _____ Use _____

b Explain why electromagnetic waves are described as being part of a spectrum.

C When infrared radiation is absorbed, it has a different effect on the body from that of ultraviolet radiation.

Describe these different effects using each of the following key words at least once:

| frequency | energy heating | ionisation | mutation | cancer |

What you need to remember

The _____ consists of seven sections of waves, each with different properties.

We can only see the _____ section; the rest are all invisible.

All are emitted by the _____. Each section has a characteristic range of _____ and frequencies. Gamma rays at one end of the spectrum have a _____ frequency, carry _____ energy, and have a short _____. Radio waves at the other end have a _____ frequency, carry _____ energy, and have a _____ wavelength. Ultra violet, X-rays, and _____ rays all carry enough energy to remove an electron from an atom and _____ it. This can cause _____ in human cells. Infrared and _____ carry less energy and cause a heating effect.

4.4.1 Modelling waves

A **a** Label the diagram using some of the key words from this list:

| amplitude | wavelength | peak or crest | trough | frequency |

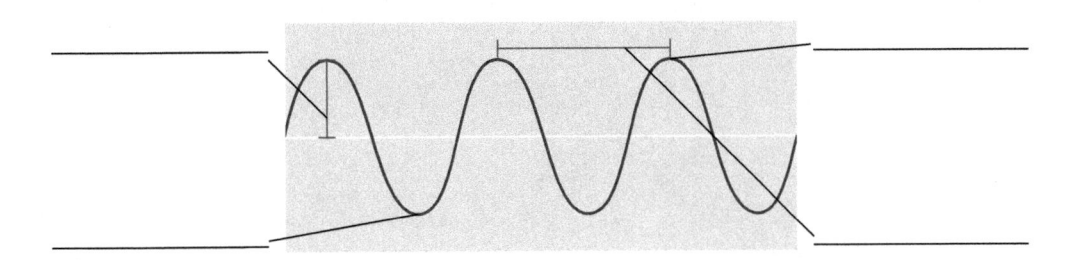

b Circle the correct **bold** word: this diagram shows a **transverse / longitudinal** wave.

B A slinky spring can be used to demonstrate many aspects of wave behaviour.

Describe how it can model:

a reflection: _____

_____

b transmission: _____

_____

c absorption: _____

_____

C Water waves can be described as transverse waves.

Describe how:

a the wave moves. _____

b an individual particle of water moves. _____

D Draw a line to match each sentence's beginning with its correct ending.

Two waves that are out of step superpose		so it reflects to produce a reflected wave.
An incident wave hits a barrier		so they add up to produce a larger wave.
Two waves that are in step superpose		so they cancel out to produce a smaller wave.

What you need to remember

In science, a _____ is an oscillation or vibration that transfers _____ or information. In a _____ wave, the oscillation is at 90° to the direction of travel of the wave. In a _____ wave, the oscillation is parallel to the direction of travel of the wave. When a wave travels through a medium it is called _____. When waves are put together they _____ – they add up or cancel out.

35

Big Idea 4 Pinchpoint

Pinchpoint question

Answer the question below, then do the follow-up activity **with the same letter** as the answer you picked.

Emelia is playing with a slinky spring, sending a wave along it. The far end is attached to a flag, which wobbles when the wave reaches it.

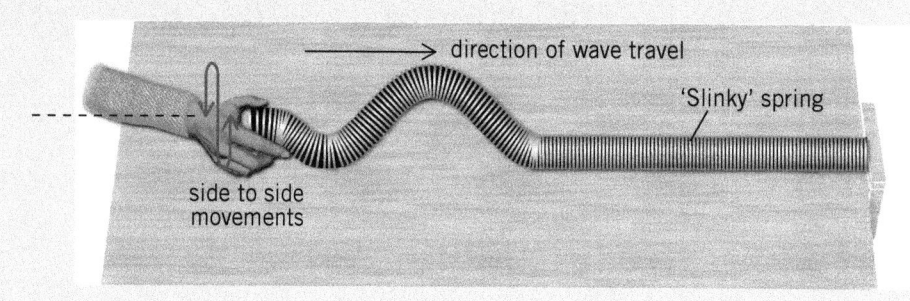

Choose the statement that best describes what is happening.

A A particle of the spring moves along the length of the spring, carrying energy with it.
B The wave is transverse because each bit of the spring oscillates at right angles to the direction that energy is transferred.
C No energy is transferred from her hand to the far end of the spring.
D The wave is longitudinal, with energy transferred along the spring.

Follow-up activities

A A transverse wave consists of a series of oscillations, which move along the wave.

   a Fill in the labels on the diagram using these keywords.

   | wavelength | energy transfer | oscillations |

   b Describe how the direction of movement of the particles in the spring relates to the direction of energy transfer.

   _____
   _____

   Hint: What direction are the oscillations in a wave? For help, see 4.4.1 Modelling waves.

B Define each type of wave below and give **one** example for each (other than in a slinky spring).

   Transverse Definition: _____
              Example: _____

   Longitudinal Definition: _____
              Example: _____

   Hint: What is the difference between a transverse and a longitudinal wave? For help, see 4.4.1 Modelling waves.

C Waves can transfer energy. Complete the sentences using these keywords to describe the situation in the Pinchpoint activity.

| work | waves | damage | along |

Energy is transmitted _____ a wave, in this case from Emelia's hand along the spring. This happens with all _____. For instance, when ocean waves crash into the shore they can cause a lot of _____ because they have transferred a lot of energy and can do a lot of _____ on the shore.

Hint: What direction is the energy transfer in a wave? For help, see 4.4.1 Modelling waves.

D a This diagram shows a sound wave, which is a longitudinal wave.

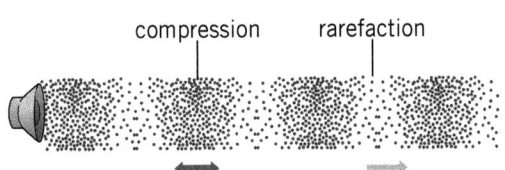

Describe how the motion of the air particles compares to the motion of the wave.

_____
_____

b This diagram shows a water wave, which is a transverse wave, moving to the right.

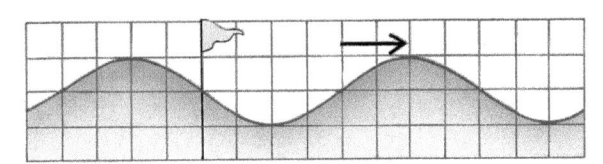

Describe how the motion of the water particles compares to the motion of the wave.

_____
_____

Hint: What is the difference between a transverse and a longitudinal wave? For help, see 4.4.1 Modelling waves.

Pinchpoint review
Now look back at the question – do you think you chose the right letter?
Turn to the Answers page to find out.

Section 1 Revision questions

1 🧪 Two sound waves in the same place at the same time will **superpose**.

  a Define the term **superpose**. *(2 marks)*

_____
_____
_____

  b Two waves meet. Circle the height (from the middle of the wave to the peak) of the resulting wave for each combination. *(2 marks)*

	Wave 1	Wave 2	Resulting wave
i	30 cm high peak	30 cm high peak	60 cm high / 30 cm high / 0 cm
ii	30 cm high peak	30 cm deep trough	60 cm high / 30 cm high / 0 cm

2 🧪 Various weights are hung from a spring.

  a It is found that the spring obeys Hooke's Law. Give the relationship between force and extension. *(1 mark)*

_____

  b The spring stretches by 2 cm when a load of 5 N is applied. Predict the extension for a load of 10 N. *(1 mark)*

_____ cm

3 🧪 **a** Tick **two** uses of electromagnets. *(2 marks)*

    1 Separating plastics for recycling ☐

    2 Motor for electrically powered train ☐

    3 Separating metal for recycling ☐

    4 Lighting with an electric light bulb ☐

  b For one of the uses you chose, describe how the electromagnet is used. *(2 marks)*

_____
_____

4 🧪 A toaster works mainly through radiation.

  a Draw a line to match each stage of the process to the object. *(3 marks)*

Transmitted through	the heating element
Absorbed by	the toast
Emitted from	the air

  b Temperature and the amount of energy in the thermal store are related to each other.

  Give the units for temperature and energy.

  Temperature _____ *(2 marks)*

  Energy _____

5 🧪 Syed is pulling his sister along on a sled over the snow. The resultant force on the sled is zero.

  a Describe the motion of the sled. *(2 marks)*

_____
_____

  b The forces are balanced partly because of the support force from the snow underneath the sled. The sled exerts stress on the snow. Syed's sister swaps to a larger sled that has the same weight.

  Tick the option that describes what happens to the stress from the sled on the snow. *(1 mark)*

    1 The stress is smaller because the weight is applied over a larger area. ☐

    2 The stress is the same because the weight has not changed. ☐

    3 The stress is larger because the weight is applied over a larger area. ☐

6 🧪 Holly decides to investigate pressure by using a pressure gauge to measure it at different depths in a swimming pool. She uses the same gauge in each measurement.

  a Tick the relationship Holly is likely to find. *(1 mark)*

    1 pressure decreases with depth ☐

    2 pressure is constant – it does not change with depth ☐

    3 pressure increases with depth ☐

b Tick any **control variables** in this experiment.
(2 marks)

Which liquid is investigated ☐

Pressure ☐

Depth ☐

Which pressure gauge is used ☐

7 a Complete this diagram to show the magnetic field lines around a bar magnet. (2 marks)

[N | S]

b Tick the statement about permanent magnets that is **wrong**. (1 mark)

All permanent magnets…

1 will cause a force on any iron placed nearby. ☐

2 have two poles. ☐

3 only emit a magnetic field when they are placed in the field of another magnet. ☐

4 will align with the Earth's magnetic field if they are free to rotate. ☐

8 A cup is stationary on a table.

Explain how the table provides a force that supports the cup. (3 marks)

_____

_____

_____

9 Waves can be either transverse or longitudinal.

a Describe the difference between transverse and longitudinal waves. (2 marks)

_____

_____

_____

_____

b A physicist is investigating the relationship between frequency and wavelength for sound waves in air. Plot the data in **Table 1** on the graph paper below, with frequency on the x-axis and wavelength on the y-axis, and draw a line of best fit. (3 marks)

Table 1

Frequency (Hz)	Wavelength (m)
40	8.6
60	5.7
80	4.3
120	2.9
160	2.1
240	1.4
320	1.1

10 A group of scientists investigating whale communication used an underwater microphone to record the sounds emitted.

Describe how the microphone detects the sounds emitted by the whales. *(3 marks)*

_____

_____

_____

11 In 2006, Hannah McKeand set the record for reaching the South Pole in the fastest time. In one hour she travelled approximately 3000 m pulling a sledge of food and equipment requiring a force of about 200 N.

Calculate the work she did in one hour and give the unit of work. The formula for calculating work done is:

work done = force × distance *(2 marks)*

_____

12 **Figure 1** shows the same gas at different temperatures.

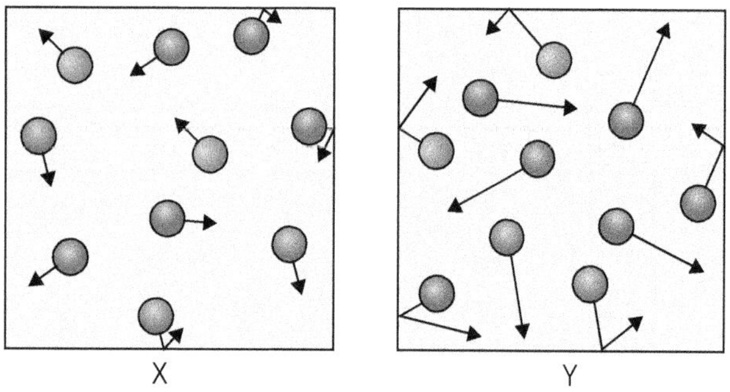

Figure 1

a i Which of these images shows a hot gas and which shows a cold gas? *(1 mark)*

Hot gas _____

Cold gas _____

ii Decide which of these images shows the gas at a higher pressure. _____ *(1 mark)*

b i In a room at room temperature, 23 °C, two balloons are refilled with air. One is filled with air at 23 °C and the other air at 80 °C.

Explain why the balloon filled with hot air will rise, whereas the balloon filled with colder air will not. *(2 marks)*

_____

_____

ii Draw a forces diagram for a balloon that is rising. *(1 mark)*

13 The pressure of a gas is important; for instance, air pressure helps us to predict the weather.

a Tick the variables that affect the pressure of a gas. *(2 marks)*

1 temperature ☐

2 electrical charge ☐

3 volume ☐

4 distance ☐

b Give the formula for calculating pressure. *(1 mark)*

_____

c Sometimes people get stuck in thick mud by rivers. A problem for firefighters when they rescue them is avoiding get stuck themselves. A firefighter has a large board to stand on, which measures 1.8 m long and 0.50 m wide.

i Calculate the area of the board. *(1 mark)*

_____

ii The firefighter has a weight of 800 N. Calculate the pressure he will exert when standing on the board and include the unit. *(2 marks)*

_____

iii If the pressure on the ground is above 20 000 N/m^2, the firefighter will sink into the mud. Explain whether he will sink if he stands on the board. *(1 mark)*

_____

_____

14 Male stag beetles have jaws 30 mm long and a strong bite of 8.0 N. A biologist studying the beetle wants to understand how they bite so strongly. Work in metres.

Calculate the moment of force and include the units. The formula for moment of force is:

moment = force × distance from pivot *(2 marks)*

_____

15 Endurance athletes, such as marathon runners, are often handed a thin, shiny blanket as they cross the finishing line.

Suggest which form of energy transfer this is mainly designed to reduce and how it does so. *(2 marks)*

16 Current in a wire acts as an electromagnet.

a Circle the option below that shows how the magnetic field strength varies with distance from the wire. *(1 mark)*

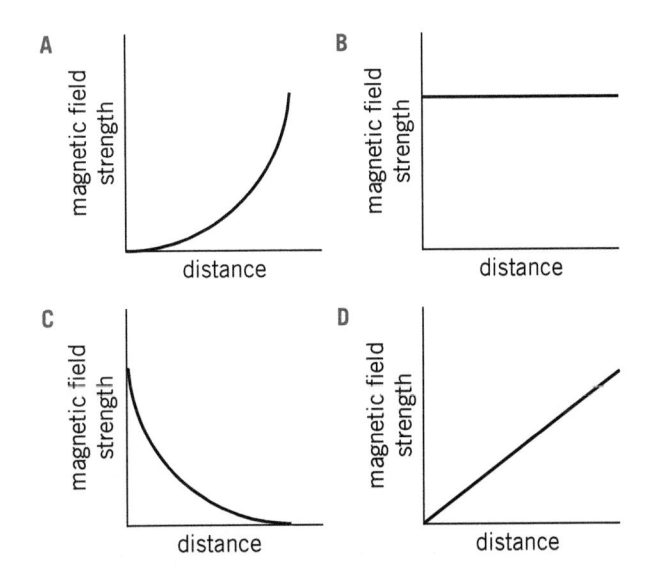

A — magnetic field strength vs distance (increasing curve)
B — magnetic field strength vs distance (constant)
C — magnetic field strength vs distance (decreasing curve)
D — magnetic field strength vs distance (linear increase)

b The loudspeaker in a pair of earphones uses electromagnetism to play music from a phone. Describe how a loudspeaker works. Draw a labelled diagram to help your description. *(6 marks)*

_____

41

Section 1 Checklist

Revision question number	Outcome	Topic reference	☹	😐	🙂
1a, b	Describe what happens when waves superpose.	4.4.1			
2a	Describe Hooke's Law of proportional stretching.	1.3.2			
2b	Use Hooke's Law to predict the extension of a spring.	1.3.2			
3a	State some uses of electromagnets.	2.4.2			
3b	Describe some uses of electromagnets.	2.4.2			
4a	State some properties of infrared radiation.	3.4.3			
4b	State how energy and temperature are measured.	3.4.1			
5a	Write down two things an object can do when the resultant force on it is zero.	1.3.1			
5b	Predict qualitatively the effect of changing area and/or force on stress.	1.4.3			
6a	State simply what happens to pressure with depth.	1.4.2			
6b	Identify control variables in an investigation.	EP6			
7a	Draw the magnetic field lines around a bar magnet.	2.3.1			
7b	Describe features of a magnet.	2.3.1			
8	Explain how solid surfaces provide a support force.	1.3.2			
9a	Compare transverse and longitudinal waves.	4.4.1			
9b	Draw an appropriate graph with a line of best fit	EP7			
10	Describe how a microphone and a loudspeaker work.	4.3.1			
11	Calculate work done.	3.3.1			
12a	Describe what happens when you heat up solids, liquids, and gases.	3.4.1			
12b	Explain why some things float and some things sink, using force diagrams.	1.4.2			
13a, b, c	Calculate fluid pressure.	1.4.1			
14	Calculate the moment of a force.	1.3.3			
15	Describe different ways to insulate in terms of conduction, convection and radiation.	3.4.3			
16a	Describe how the magnetic field strength due to a current carrying wire varies with distance from the wire.	2.4.1			
16b	Describe how an electric bell, circuit breaker, or loudspeaker works.	2.4.2			

5.3.1 Elements

A Each sentence below has one mistake. Read the sentences and correct the mistakes.
1. Every material, and everything in the Universe, is made up of two or more elements.
2. It is easy to break down an element into other substances.
3. The chemical symbol of magnesium is MG.
4. The chemical symbol of sodium is nA.
5. Scientists in the UK and Russia use different symbols for the element iron.

B Draw a line to match each element name with its chemical symbol.

Element	Chemical symbol
aluminium	Cl
bromine	Br
carbon	Au
chlorine	H
copper	Fe
gold	C
hydrogen	I
iodine	Cu
iron	Al

C Complete the table, filling in the names of the elements and their chemical symbols.

Name of element	Chemical symbol
	K
magnesium	
nitrogen	
	Na
oxygen	
sulfur	
	W
zinc	

What you need to remember

An element is a substance that cannot be broken down into other _____. There are 98 naturally occurring _____, and they are all listed in the _____ Table. Every element has its own _____ symbol, which is a one- or two-letter code for the element. Scientists all over the world use the same chemical _____ for the elements.

5.3.2 Atoms

A Draw a line to match each sentence starter to one ending. You do not need to use all the endings.

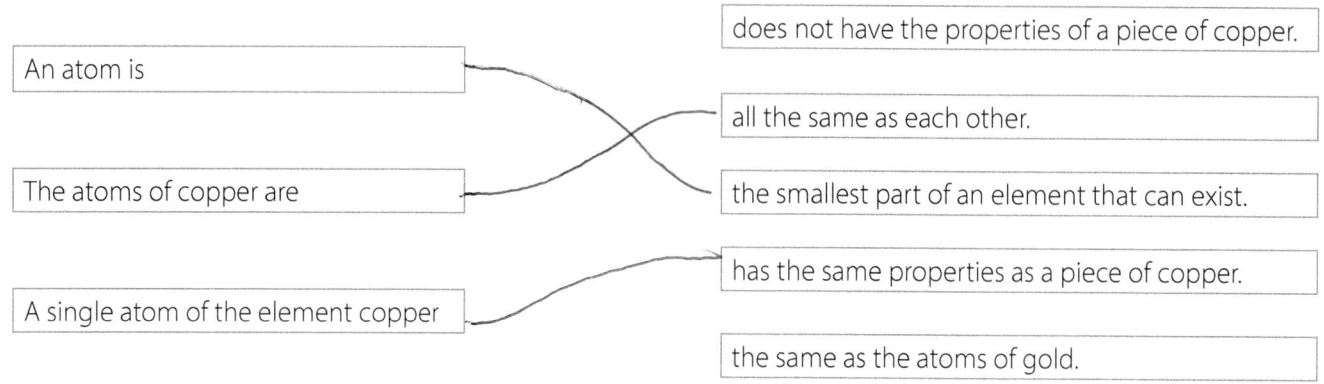

An atom is	does not have the properties of a piece of copper.
	all the same as each other.
The atoms of copper are	the smallest part of an element that can exist.
	has the same properties as a piece of copper.
A single atom of the element copper	the same as the atoms of gold.

Matches drawn:
- An atom is → the smallest part of an element that can exist.
- The atoms of copper are → all the same as each other.
- A single atom of the element copper → does not have the properties of a piece of copper.

B The diagrams show four different substances. Two of the substances are elements and two are not. Each circle is one atom. The white, light grey, and dark grey atoms are different from each other.

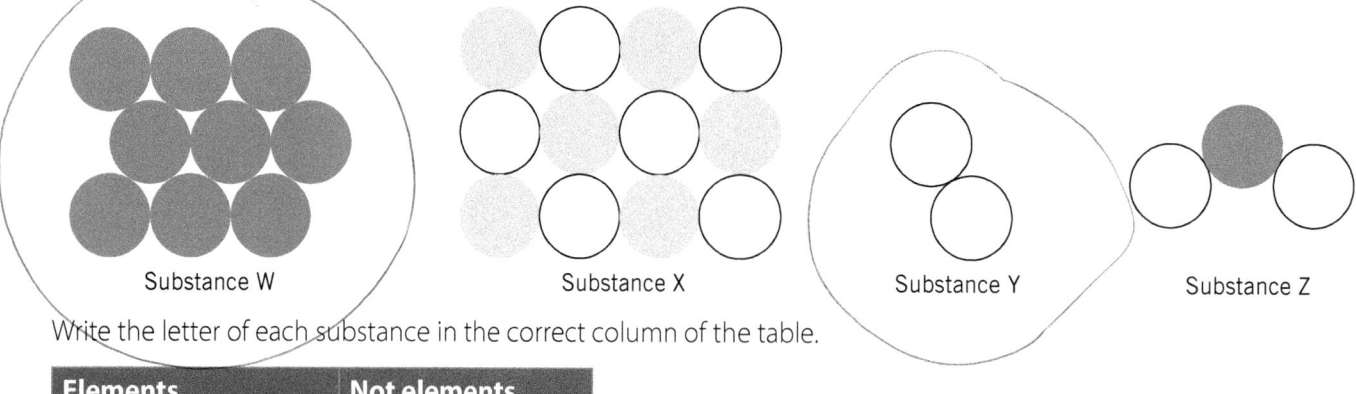

Substance W — Substance X — Substance Y — Substance Z

Write the letter of each substance in the correct column of the table.

Elements	Not elements
Y W	X Z

Hint: Every element has its own type of atom, so if a substance has more than one type of atom, it is not an element.

C The table shows data about the atoms of three elements.

Element	Radius of atom (nm)	Relative mass of atom
copper	0.128	64
mercury	0.152	201
zinc	0.133	65

Circle the correct **bold** words in the sentences below.

Of the elements in the table, copper has the atoms with the **biggest / (smallest)** mass. The element that has atoms with the greatest mass is **copper / (mercury) / zinc**. The element with the biggest atoms in the table is **copper / (mercury) / zinc**. Mercury is shiny, and it is liquid at room temperature. These properties are the properties of **(one) / many** mercury atom(s).

Hint: The radius of an atom shows its size. The greater the radius, the bigger the atom.

What you need to remember

Elements are made up of ____atoms____. An atom is the ____smallest____ part of an element that can exist. All the ____atoms____ of an element are the same. The atoms of one element are ____different____ from the atoms of all the other elements. The properties of an element are the properties of ____several____ atoms joined together.

5.3.3 Compounds

A Write one key word next to each definition. Choose from the key words in the box below.

| element | compound | molecule | atom |

Definition	Key word
A substance that is made of atoms of two or more elements joined together strongly.	
A substance that cannot be broken down into other substances. It is made of one type of atom.	
The smallest part of an element that can exist.	
A particle that is made up of two or more atoms strongly joined together.	

B Circle the correct **bold** words in the sentences below.

Iron is made up of one type of atom, so it is **an element / a compound**. Sulfur is also made up of one type of atom, so it is **an element / a compound**.

Iron sulfide is made up of atoms of **two / three** elements, iron and sulfur. This means that iron sulfide is **an element / a compound**. The properties of iron sulfide are **the same as / different from** the properties of iron and sulfur. For example, sulfur is **yellow / grey** but iron sulfide is **yellow / grey**, and iron is **magnetic / not magnetic** but iron sulfide is **magnetic / not magnetic**. This is because, in iron sulfide, iron and sulfur atoms are **joined / mixed** together to make one substance.

C The diagrams show some molecules.
The grey circles represent atoms of one element and the white circles represent atoms of another element.

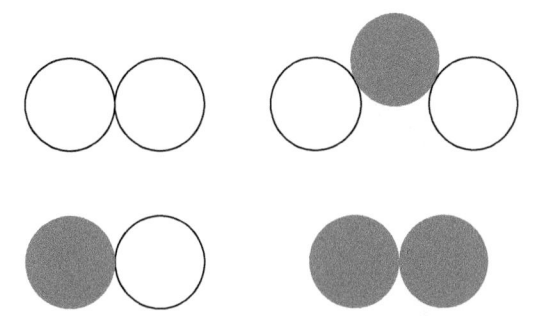

a   Use a **pencil** to draw a ring around the two molecules that represent elements.
b   Use a **pen** to draw a ring around the two molecules that represent compounds.

What you need to remember

A compound is a substance that is made up of atoms of _____ or more elements. The atoms are _____ joined together. The properties of a compound are _____ from the properties of the elements whose atoms are in it because the atoms are joined together to make _____ substance. A _____ is a group of atoms that are joined together strongly.

5.3.4 Chemical formulae

A Draw a line to match each compound name to its chemical formula and to the elements whose atoms are in the compound.

Compound name	Chemical formula	Elements whose atoms are in the compound
magnesium oxide	CO_2	sulfur and chlorine
sodium chloride	SCl_2	magnesium and oxygen
carbon dioxide	NaCl	carbon and oxygen
sulfur dichloride	MgO	calcium, sulfur, and oxygen
calcium sulfate	$CaSO_4$	sodium and chlorine

B The diagrams show some molecules of elements and compounds. Write the correct chemical formula next to each diagram.

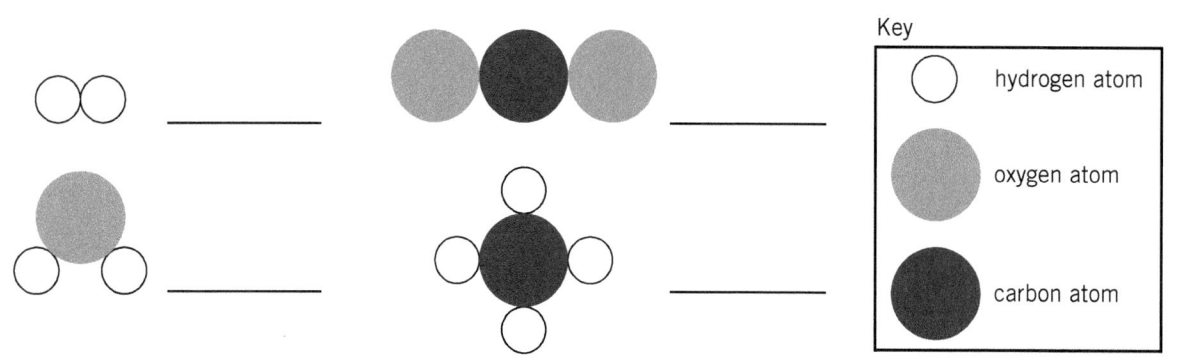

Key:
- hydrogen atom
- oxygen atom
- carbon atom

C Many compounds contain carbon, hydrogen, oxygen, and nitrogen atoms. Some of their formulae are in the table. For each compound, write down the number of atoms of each element shown in the formula. The first one has been done for you.

Name of compound	Formula of compound	Number of carbon atoms	Number of hydrogen atoms	Number of oxygen atoms	Number of nitrogen atoms
methane (in natural gas)	CH_4	1	4	0	0
ethanoic acid (in vinegar)	$C_2H_4O_2$				
ethanol (in alcoholic drinks)	C_2H_6O				
paracetamol (a painkiller)	$C_8H_9NO_2$				
ibuprofen (a painkiller)	$C_{13}H_{18}O_2$				

What you need to remember

A _____ formula uses chemical symbols to show the elements in a substance. It also shows the number of atoms of one element compared to the _____ of atoms of another element. For example, the chemical formula of water is H_2O. This shows that water is made up of two elements – hydrogen and _____. It also shows that there are two atoms of hydrogen for every _____ atom of oxygen.

5.3.5 Polymers

A The sentences below are about polymers. There is one mistake in each sentence. Copy out each sentence, correcting its mistake.

A polymer is a substance with very short molecules.

A polymer molecule has many different groups of atoms, joined together in a long chain.

There are 10 different polymers.

Methane, CH_4, melts at a lower temperature than poly(ethene) because methane has bigger molecules than poly(ethene).

B Draw a line from each use of a polymer to the statement that **best** describes how its properties make it suitable for this use.

Poly(propene) is used to make ropes	because it is strong and flexible, does not wear away, and is not damaged by blood.
Nylon can be used to make artificial heart valves	because it is strong and lightweight.
Cotton is used to make clothes	because it can be spun into flexible threads that can be woven into cloth.
Kevlar® is used to make bullet-proof vests that police officers can wear all day	because it is strong and flexible.

C The table gives data for three polymers.
Choose the **two** polymers in the table that are suitable for making water bottles.
Give a reason for your choice.

Name of polymer	Is it waterproof?	Density (g/cm³)	Flexibility
LDPE	yes	0.92	very flexible
PETE	yes	1.38	rigid
Rigid PVC	yes	1.30	rigid
Poly(propene)	yes	0.90	very flexible

Polymer names _____ and _____

Reason _____

What you need to remember

A polymer is a substance with very _____ molecules. Its molecules have identical groups of atoms, repeated _____ times. There are _____ polymers, each with _____ properties. The properties of polymers depend on the groups of _____ in their molecules.

5.4.1 The Periodic Table

A The table shows the melting points of the elements in Group 1 of the Periodic Table.
Plot the melting point values on a bar chart, using these axes.

Element	Melting point (°C)
lithium	180
sodium	98
potassium	64
rubidium	39

B Circle the correct **bold** words in the sentences below.
Use data from the table in activity **A** to help you, and the Periodic Table.

Lithium is at the **top / bottom** of Group 1, and rubidium is near the **top / bottom** of the group. From top to bottom of the group, the melting point **increases / decreases**. The element caesium is **above / below** rubidium in Group 1. A sensible prediction for the melting point of caesium is **29 / 49** °C.

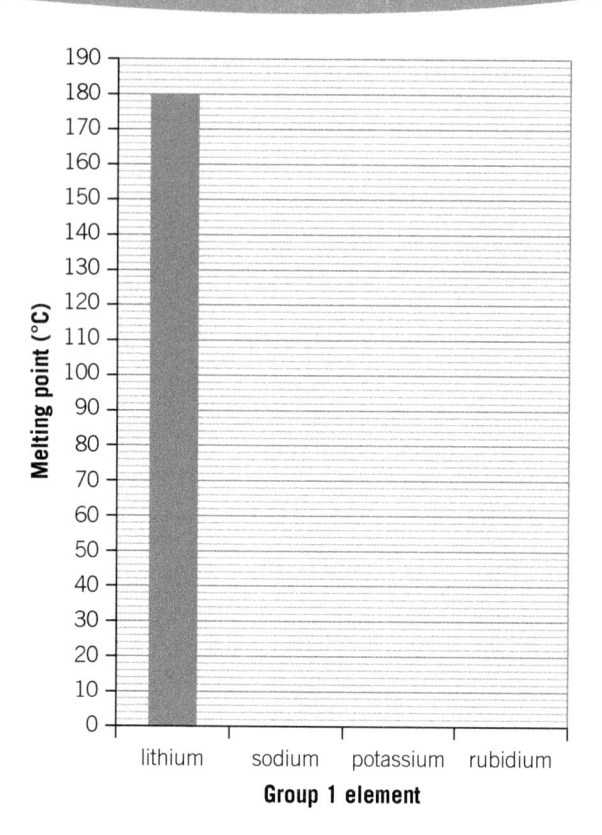

C The tables shows the densities of some Group 3 and Group 4 elements. Boron is at the top of Group 3 of the Periodic Table, and carbon is at the top of Group 4.

Group 3 element	Density (g/cm³)
boron	2.3
aluminium	2.7
gallium	5.9
indium	7.3
thallium	11.8

Group 4 element	Density (g/cm³)
carbon	2.2
silicon	2.3
germanium	5.3
tin	7.3
lead	11.3

Draw a line from each sentence starter to **one** correct ending.
You can use each ending once, twice, or not at all.

From top to bottom of Group 3,	similar for Group 3 and Group 4.
From top to bottom of Group 4,	density increases.
The pattern in density is	different for Group 3 and Group 4.
From bottom to top of Group 4,	density decreases.

What you need to remember

In the Periodic Table, the vertical columns are called _____ and the horizontal rows are called _____. There are patterns in the properties of the elements down _____ and across _____. You can use patterns in the melting point of the elements in a _____ to predict the melting point of an element whose melting point you do not know.

5.4.2 The elements of Group 1

A Mr Guthrie adds some universal indicator to a big container of water. He adds a small piece of potassium, and there is a vigorous reaction. Label the diagram using the words provided.

| water and universal indicator | potassium | purple flame | bubbles of gas |

B Each sentence below has one mistake. Read the sentences and correct the mistakes.

The Group 1 elements have very different reactions with water.

When any Group 1 element reacts with water, oxygen gas is made.

From top to bottom of Group 1, the reactions of the elements with water get less vigorous.

Rubidium is below potassium in Group 1, so the reaction of rubidium with water is less vigorous.

The reaction of potassium with water is a physical property of potassium.

Melting point is a chemical property.

From top to bottom of Group 1, there is not a pattern in melting points.

C The table shows the atomic radius of some elements in Group 1. The elements in the table are shown in the same order as they are in the Periodic Table. The greater the atomic radius, the bigger the atom.
Circle the correct **bold** words and phrases in the sentences below.

Element	Atomic radius (nm)
sodium	0.19
potassium	0.23
rubidium	0.25

Going down Group 1, the atomic radius **increases / decreases**. Lithium is at the top of Group 1, above sodium. The pattern suggests that the atomic radius of lithium is **less than / more than** the atomic radius of sodium. Caesium is below rubidium in Group 1. The pattern suggests that its atomic radius could be **0.21 / 0.26** nm.

What you need to remember

Group 1 contains the elements in the column on the _____ of the Periodic Table. The elements in Group 1 are also called the _____ metals. They _____ electricity and are _____ when freshly cut. The Group 1 elements have similar chemical properties.
For example, they react _____ with water. When a Group 1 element reacts with water, _____ substances are made. These substances are _____ gas and a metal _____.

49

5.4.3 The elements of Group 7

A Mrs Hull is using bromine to do an experiment. The bottle of bromine has two hazard symbols.
Draw a line to match each hazard symbol to its meaning, a risk from the hazard, and how to control the risk.

Hazard symbol	Meaning	Risk from this hazard	How to control the risk
(skull and crossbones)	toxic	burns eyes	use in a fume cupboard, so that any fumes from the liquid do not go into the room
(corrosive symbol)	corrosive	difficulty breathing	wear safety goggles

B The table shows some data for Group 7. Fluorine is at the top of the group.

Element	State at room temperature	Colour at room temperature
fluorine	gas	pale yellow
chlorine	gas	green
bromine	liquid	dark red
iodine	solid	grey-black

Circle the correct **bold** words in the sentences below. Use data from the table to help you.

The colours of the Group 7 elements get **lighter / darker** going down the group. The elements at the **top / bottom** of the group are in the gas state at room temperature. Astatine is at the bottom of Group 7, below **fluorine / iodine**. This means that it is sensible to predict that astatine is in the **solid / liquid / gas** state at room temperature and that its colour is **dark / light**.

C Mrs Hull adds chlorine solution to sodium bromide solution. Her observations are in the table.

Solution	Appearance
chlorine solution (before reaction)	pale green
sodium bromide solution (before reaction)	colourless
mixture after reaction	yellow-orange

Tick the statements about the experiment that are true.

1. The products of the reaction are sodium chloride and bromine ☐
2. The reaction is a displacement reaction. ☐
3. Chlorine is less reactive than bromine. ☐
4. Chlorine displaces bromine from sodium bromide. ☐

What you need to remember

Group 7 contains the elements in the column that is second from the _____ of the Periodic Table. The elements in Group 7 are also called the _____. They are non-_____. The Group 7 elements have similar reactions, and show a _____ in reactivity. The Group 7 elements take part in displacement _____. In one of these, chlorine reacts with sodium bromide to make sodium _____ and bromine. In this reaction, chlorine _____ bromine from one of its compounds.

5.4.4 The elements of Group 0

A Choose the letters of the **three** correct statements that describe the elements in Group 0.

The elements in Group 0… _____ _____ _____

- **U** are unreactive.
- **V** are in the gas state at room temperature.
- **W** are in the solid state at room temperature.
- **X** are called the halogens.
- **Y** react vigorously with water.
- **Z** are called the noble gases.

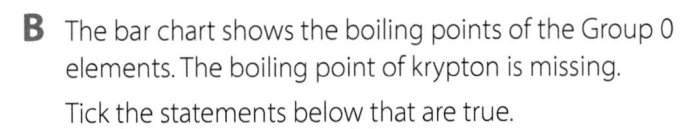

B The bar chart shows the boiling points of the Group 0 elements. The boiling point of krypton is missing.

Tick the statements below that are true.

1. All the noble gases have boiling points above 0 °C. ☐
2. The boiling point of argon is higher than the boiling point of neon. ☐
3. The boiling point of argon is lower than the boiling point of neon. ☐
4. From helium at the top of Group 0 to xenon at the bottom, boiling point increases. ☐
5. Boiling point decreases from top to bottom of Group 0. ☐
6. From the pattern shown, a sensible prediction for the boiling point of krypton is −152 °C. ☐

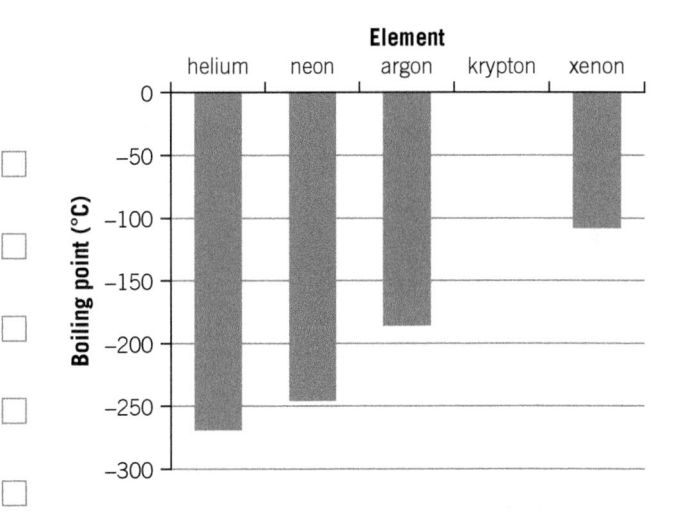

C The table gives the density of each Group 0 element, and air.

a Write the chemical symbols of the elements in order of **decreasing** density, highest density first.

_____

_____

Element	Chemical symbol	Density in kg/m³ at 0 °C
helium	He	0.2
neon	Ne	0.9
argon	Ar	1.8
krypton	Kr	3.7
xenon	Xe	5.9
air	–	1.3

b Each Group 0 element is used to fill a separate balloon.

Predict which balloons fall to the ground when dropped in air.

_____

Hint: Balloons filled with a gas that is more dense than air fall, and balloons filled with a gas that is less dense than air rise.

What you need to remember

Group 0 contains the elements in the column on the _____ of the Periodic Table. The elements in Group 0 are also called the _____ gases. They are non-_____. Most Group 0 elements do not take part in chemical reactions – in other words, they are _____.

51

Big Idea 5 Pinchpoint

Pinchpoint question

Answer the question below, then do the follow-up activity **with the same letter** as the answer you picked.

Look at these elements in Group 1 and Group 7 of the Periodic Table.

Every Group 1 element can react with every Group 7 element.
Which pair of elements reacts most vigorously, and why?

A Sodium and chlorine because they are both very reactive elements.

B Caesium and fluorine because the Group 1 elements are more reactive from top to bottom but the Group 7 elements get less reactive from top to bottom.

C Potassium and chlorine because potassium is more reactive than the elements above it and chlorine is more reactive than the elements below it.

D Caesium and iodine because the Group 1 elements get more reactive from top to bottom and the same is true for all other groups.

Follow-up activities

A In Group 1, elements get **more** reactive from top to bottom. In Group 7, elements get **less** reactive from top to bottom.

   a Circle the correct **bold** words in the sentences below.

      The patterns in reactivity for groups 1 and 7 are **the same / different**. Caesium is at the **top / bottom** of **Group 1 / Group 7**. This means that caesium is the **most / least** reactive element in this group. Lithium is at the **top / bottom** of **Group 1 / Group 7**. This means that lithium is the **most / least** reactive element in this group. Fluorine is at the **top / bottom** of **Group 1 / Group 7**. This means that fluorine is the **most / least** reactive element in this group. Iodine is near the **top / bottom** of **Group 1 / Group 7**. This means that iodine is **more / less** reactive than fluorine, chlorine, and bromine.

   b Complete the word equations below. Then circle the correct **bold** words in the sentences below the equations.

      iron + chlorine → _____ chloride

      iron + _____ → iron bromide

      _____ + iodine → iron _____

      The most vigorous of these three reactions is the reaction between iron and **chlorine / iodine**. This is because **chlorine / iodine** is the most reactive of the Group 7 elements in these reactions.

c Complete the word equations below. Then circle the correct **bold** words in the sentences below the equations.

lithium + water → lithium hydroxide + _____

sodium + _____ → sodium hydroxide + hydrogen

potassium + water → _____ _____ + hydrogen

The least vigorous of these three reactions is the reaction between **lithium / potassium** and water. This is

because **lithium / potassium** is the least reactive of the Group 1 elements in these reactions.

Hint: In Group 1, the most reactive element is at the bottom of the group, and in Group 7 the most reactive element is at the top of the group. Which is the most reactive element in Group 1? For help, see 5.4.2 The elements of Group 1 and 5.4.3 The elements of Group 7.

B Look at the lists of elements in Group 2 and Group 7. The elements are in the same order as in the Periodic Table.

Group 2

| beryllium |
| magnesium |
| calcium |
| strontium |
| barium |

Group 7

| fluorine |
| chlorine |
| bromine |
| iodine |

In Group 2, the elements get **more** reactive from top to bottom, just like Group 1.

In Group 7, the elements get **less** reactive from top to bottom.

a List the pairs of elements below in decreasing order of how vigorously they react, **most reactive first**.

Correct order ☐ ☐ ☐ ☐

1 beryllium and iodine

2 barium and fluorine

3 barium and chlorine

4 magnesium and iodine

b i Complete the word equations below.

calcium + iodine → _____ iodide

calcium + bromine → _____ _____

strontium + bromine → _____ _____

ii Circle the word equation that represents the most vigorous of the three reactions.

Hint: The most vigorous reaction is between the most reactive elements in each group. Which is the most reactive element in Group 7? For help, see 5.4.3 The elements of Group 7.

C In Group 1, elements get **more** reactive from top to bottom. In Group 7, elements get **less** reactive from top to bottom.

a Tick the statements below that are true. Consider only the elements whose names and chemical symbols are shown in the Periodic Table above in the Pinchpoint question.

1 The most vigorous reaction is between caesium and iodine. ☐

2 The least vigorous reaction is between lithium and iodine. ☐

3 The reaction of lithium and fluorine is more vigorous than the reaction of sodium and fluorine. ☐

4 The reaction of caesium and bromine is more vigorous than the reaction of caesium and iodine. ☐

5 The reaction of lithium and fluorine is less vigorous than the reaction of potassium and fluorine. ☐
6 The reaction of rubidium and iodine is more vigorous than the reaction of rubidium and chlorine. ☐

b Now write corrected versions of the three statements that are not true.

_____

_____

_____

Hint: The most vigorous reaction is between the most reactive element in Group 1 and the most reactive element in Group 7. Which is the most reactive element in Group 1? For help, see 5.4.2 The elements of Group 1 and 5.4.3 The elements of Group 7.

D The patterns in reactivity are different for different groups of the Periodic Table:

In Groups 1 and 2, the elements get **more** reactive from top to bottom.
In Group 7, the elements get **less** reactive from top to bottom.

Draw a line to match each element name to its position in its group and to its relative reactivity.

Element	Position and group	Relative reactivity
Lithium	is at the top of Group 1	so it is the least reactive element in its group.
Fluorine	is at the bottom of Group 1	
Caesium	is at the top of Group 7	so it is the most reactive element in its group.
Iodine	is near the bottom of Group 7	

Hint: In Group 1, the most reactive element is at the bottom of the Group, and in Group 7, the most reactive element is at the top of the Group. For help, see 5.4.2 The elements of Group 1 and 5.4.3 The elements of Group 7.

Pinchpoint review

Now look back at the question – do you think you chose the right letter?
Turn to the Answers page to find out.

6.3.1 Atoms in chemical reactions

A Complete the word equations for the reactions described below.

   a Sulfur burns in oxygen to make sulfur dioxide.

      sulfur + _____ → sulfur dioxide

   b Sodium reacts with chlorine to make sodium chloride.

      sodium + _____ → sodium _____

   c Methane burns in oxygen to make carbon dioxide and water.

      methane + _____ → _____ _____ + _____

B The particle diagram below represents the reaction of hydrogen with oxygen. It shows how the atoms are joined together before and after the reaction.

hydrogen oxygen   water

   a Name the two reactants in the reaction.

      _____ and _____

   b Name the product in the reaction.

      _____

   c Write down the number of hydrogen atoms shown in the reactants. ____

   d Write down the number of hydrogen atoms shown in the products. ____

   e Write down the number of oxygen atoms shown in the reactants. ____

   f Write down the number of oxygen atoms shown in the products. ____

Hint: In a word equation or particle diagram, the reactants are shown on the left of the arrow, and the products are shown on the right of the arrow.

C Tick the statement or statements that are **true** for any chemical reaction.

   1 The total number of atoms increases. ☐
   2 The atoms are rearranged. ☐
   3 The atoms are joined together in the same way before and after the reaction. ☐
   4 The number of atoms of each element is conserved. ☐

What you need to remember

In a chemical reaction, the starting substances are the _____, and the substances that are made are the _____. Word equations represent chemical reactions. In a word equation, the reactants are on the _____ of the arrow and the products are on the _____. In a chemical reaction, _____ are rearranged. The atoms are joined together _____ before and after the reaction. There are the same number of atoms of each element before and _____ the reaction; in other words, atoms are conserved.

6.3.2 Combustion

A Draw a line to match each word to its definition.

fuel	a fuel that cannot be replaced once it has been used
combustion	a material that burns to transfer energy by heating
renewable fuel	a reaction with oxygen in which energy is transferred to the surroundings as heat and light
non-renewable fuel	a fuel that can be produced over a short timescale

B The products of a combustion reaction are the substances that are made when a substance burns. Complete the table with the names of the products of combustion.

Fuel	Product or products of combustion
carbon	
hydrogen	
butane (a compound of carbon and hydrogen that is used in camping stoves)	

C Riley does an investigation to compare the increase in temperature of water when two different fuels burn. Here is a diagram of the apparatus. The fuels are wax and ethanol.

  a The list below shows the variables in the investigation. **Circle** the independent variable. Draw a **box** around the dependent variable. **Underline** the **two** control variables.

  volume of water   **fuel**

  increase in temperature of water   **distance of flame from test tube**

  b Riley wants to draw a results table for her experiment.

  i Write down the column heading for the column on the **left** of her table. _____

  ii Write down the column heading for the column on the **right** of her table. _____

  Hint: The independent variable is in the left column, and the dependent variable is in the right column.

What you need to remember

A fuel is a material that burns to transfer _____ by heating. The scientific word for burning is _____. When a fuel burns it reacts with _____ from the air. The product of combustion of carbon is _____. The products of combustion of a fuel that is made from carbon and hydrogen atoms are carbon dioxide and _____.

56

6.3.3 Thermal decomposition

A Tick the statements below that are **true**.

1. In a decomposition reaction, a compound breaks down. ☐
2. Every decomposition reaction has two or more products. ☐
3. The products of a decomposition reaction are always elements. ☐
4. In a decomposition reaction, there is one reactant only. ☐
5. In a decomposition reaction, the total number of atoms of each element is the same in the reactants and products. ☐

B Raj heats copper carbonate in the apparatus shown in the diagram.

He writes the time for the limewater to start looking cloudy in the table below.

He then repeats the experiment with two more compounds.

Compound	Time for limewater to start looking cloudy (minutes)
copper carbonate	1
potassium carbonate	did not go cloudy after heating for 10 minutes
lead carbonate	4

Draw a line to match each compound with the correct statement about its decomposition. Use the information in the table to help you.

copper carbonate		did not decompose
lead carbonate		decomposed most quickly
potassium carbonate		decomposed more slowly than copper carbonate

C Highlight or underline the **two** word equations that show decomposition reactions.

a W calcium carbonate → calcium oxide + carbon dioxide
   X magnesium + nitrogen → magnesium nitride
   Y methane + oxygen → carbon dioxide + water
   Z sodium nitrate → sodium nitrite + oxygen

b Explain why the reactions you chose in part **a** are decomposition reactions.

_____

What you need to remember

In a decomposition reaction, _____ reactant breaks down to make _____ or more products. The reactant must be a _____. The products can be elements or _____.

Zinc carbonate, for example, decomposes to make zinc _____ and _____

_____. When heat is needed to make a substance break down, the reaction is called a

_____ decomposition reaction.

6.3.4 Conservation of mass

A Circle the correct **bold** words and phrases in the sentences below.

In a chemical reaction, the total mass of the reactants is **equal to / greater than** the total mass of the products.

In a physical change, such as **melting / burning**, the total mass **increases / does not change**. This is the law of **combustion / conservation** of mass.

B Hydrogen and oxygen react together to make water.

hydrogen + oxygen → water

The diagrams show some of the atoms before and after the reaction.

Complete the sentence below:

The total mass of hydrogen and oxygen that reacts is the same as the mass of water made because

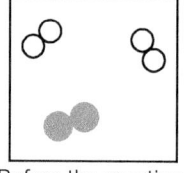

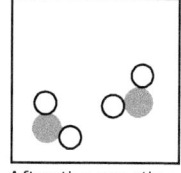

_____

_____

Before the reaction   After the reaction

C Anna finds the mass of some magnesium. Then she sets up the apparatus shown.

She lights the Bunsen burner and heats the crucible, opening the lid every now and again.

She stops heating and waits for everything to cool.

Then she finds the mass of the product. Her results are in the table.

Substance	Is this substance a reactant or product?	Mass of substance (g)
magnesium	reactant	0.12
magnesium oxide	product	0.20

The word equation for the reaction is

magnesium + oxygen → magnesium oxide

Circle the correct **bold** words and phrases in the sentences below.

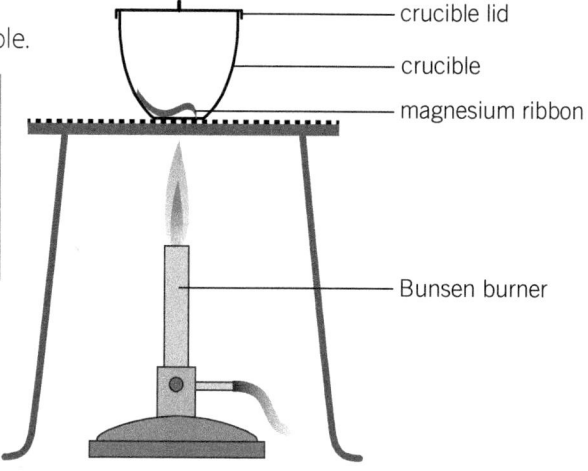

In Anna's experiment, the solid reactant is **magnesium / magnesium oxide**, of mass 0.12 g. The product is **magnesium / magnesium oxide**, of mass 0.20 g. The mass of solid has **decreased / increased**. This means that magnesium reacts with a **gas / solid** from the air – oxygen. The total mass of the two reactants, magnesium and oxygen, is **the same as / less than** the mass of the product, magnesium oxide. This means that the mass of oxygen that reacts is 0.20 g – 0.12 g = **0.32 g / 0.08 g**.

What you need to remember

In a chemical reaction, the atoms are rearranged and _____ together differently. The number and mass of each type of atom does not _____. This means that in a chemical reaction, the total mass of products is _____ to the total mass of reactants. This is the law of _____ of mass.

Mass is also conserved in _____ changes.

6.4.1 Exothermic and endothermic

A Barney sets up the apparatus opposite.

He pours dilute hydrochloric acid into the cup, and measures its temperature.

Then he adds a piece of magnesium ribbon. There is a chemical reaction.

At the end of the chemical reaction he measures the temperature again.

Then Barney repeats the experiment with zinc instead of magnesium.

Some of his results are in the table. Complete the table by filling in the empty boxes.

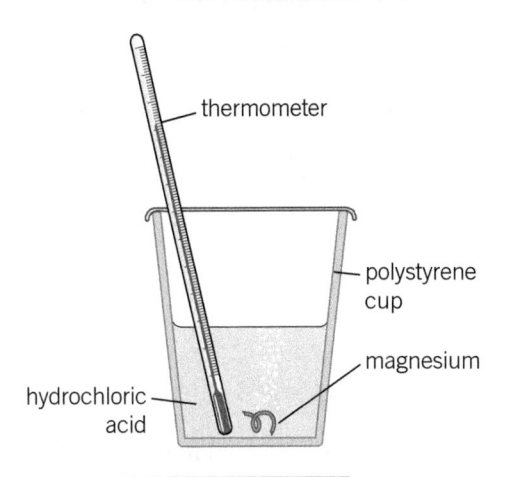

Reacting substances	Temperature before the reaction (°C)	Temperature after the reaction (°C)	Temperature change (°C)
hydrochloric acid and magnesium	20	28	
hydrochloric acid and zinc	20		5

B The sentences below are about Barney's experiment in activity **A**. Circle the correct **bold** words.

The temperatures of both reacting mixtures **decrease / increase**. This means that the reactions are **exothermic / endothermic**. The temperature change for the reaction with magnesium is **less / more** than the temperature change for the reaction with zinc. This means that the reaction with magnesium is **less / more** exothermic.

C Complete the table by identifying whether each of the changes listed are chemical reactions or physical changes, and whether the changes are exothermic or endothermic.

	Description of change	chemical reaction or physical change?	exothermic or endothermic?
1	When a cold pack is activated, ammonium nitrate dissolves in water.		
2	Burning candle wax transfers energy from the reaction mixture to the surroundings.		
3	Citric acid reacts with sodium hydrogen carbonate to make new substances. The reacting mixture feels colder than the starting substances.		

What you need to remember

Chemical reactions involve _____ transfers. If the temperature increases, the reaction is _____, and energy is _____ from the reaction mixture to the surroundings. If the temperature decreases, the reaction is _____, and energy is transferred from the _____ to the reaction mixture. Physical changes also involve _____ transfers. In an exothermic change, energy is transferred _____ the surroundings. In an endothermic change, energy is transferred _____ the surroundings.

6.4.2 Energy level diagrams

A The energy level diagram below represents the energy change when liquid oxygen boils.

Tick the statements that are **true** for the change shown in the diagram.
1. Liquid oxygen stores more energy than the same amount of oxygen gas. ☐
2. The substance at the start stores less energy than the substance at the end. ☐
3. During the change, energy is transferred from the surroundings to the boiling oxygen. ☐
4. The change is exothermic. ☐

B The solid line in the diagram shows the energy stored in the reactants in an exothermic chemical reaction.

Write down the letter of the dotted line that could represent the energy stored by the products of the reaction.

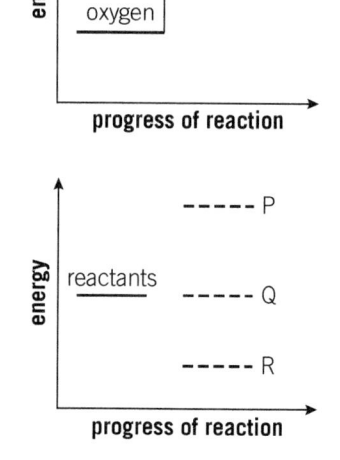

_____

C The table shows the energy transferred when three different fuels burn.

Fuel	Energy stored by fuel (kJ/g)	Energy level diagram
ethanol	27	
hydrogen	120	
petrol	44	

The energy level diagrams show the energy transferred to the surroundings when 1 g of each of the fuels in the table burns. The diagrams are all drawn to the same scale.

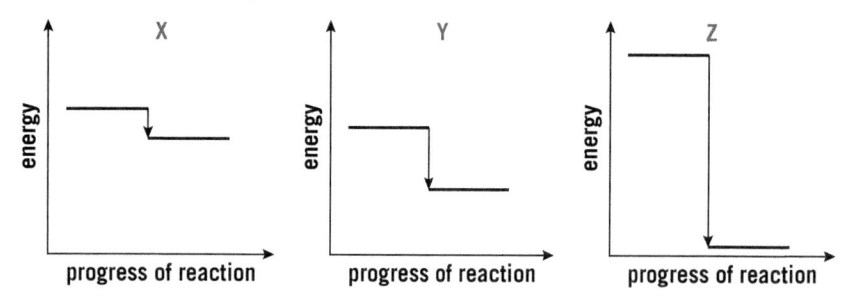

In each empty box in the table, write down the letter of the energy diagram that represents the named fuel.

What you need to remember

An energy level diagram for a chemical reaction shows the relative amounts of energy stored in the reactants and _____. An energy level diagram for a physical change shows the relative amounts of energy in the substance before and _____ the change. In an energy level diagram, if the horizontal line on the left is higher, the reaction is _____. If the horizontal line on the left is lower, the reaction is _____.

6.4.3 Bond energies

A Complete the table by drawing one tick in each row and writing down whether each change is exothermic or endothermic.

	Particle diagram to represent process	✓ if the process requires energy from the surroundings	✓ if the process transfers energy to the surroundings	Is the process exothermic or endothermic?
a	●● ⟶ ● + ●			
b	● + ● ⟶ ●●			

B The energy level diagram below represents the chemical reaction of nitrogen with oxygen to make nitrogen monoxide.

In each box on the diagram, write the letter of the correct label.

Labels

X   overall energy change for the reaction

Y   energy given out when new bonds are made

Z   energy need to break bonds

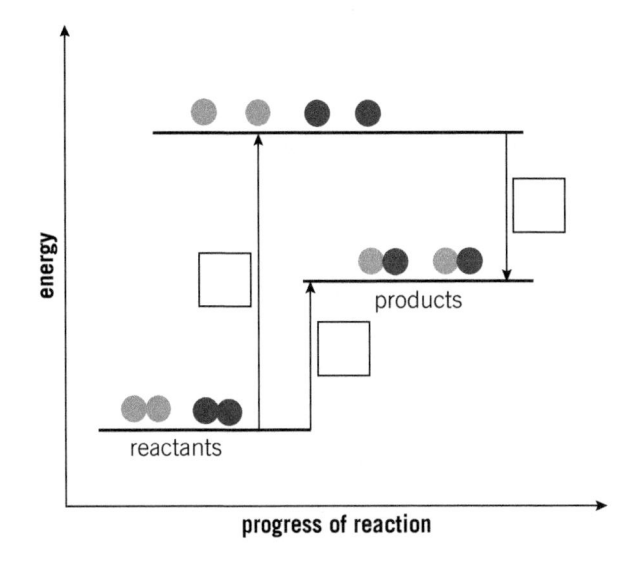

C The sentences below are about the energy level diagram in activity **B**.

Circle the correct **bold** words.

The energy level diagram shows that the energy needed to break bonds in this reaction is **less / more** than the energy given out when the new bonds are made. This means that, overall, the chemical reaction transfers energy **to / from** the surroundings. The reaction is **endothermic / exothermic**.

What you need to remember

A chemical reaction starts when bonds between atoms in the reactants _____. This process requires energy from the surroundings, so is _____. Then new bonds form between atoms to make the _____. This process transfers energy to the surroundings, so is _____. Overall, a chemical reaction is endothermic if the energy required to break bonds is _____ than the energy released in making new bonds. A reaction is exothermic if the energy required to break bonds is _____ than the energy released in making new bonds. A substance that speeds up a chemical reaction without being changed itself is a _____.

Big Idea 6 Pinchpoint

Pinchpoint question

Answer the question below, then do the follow-up activity **with the same letter** as the answer you picked.

The diagrams show atoms of the reactants and product before and after the combustion reaction of carbon.

Which statement about the reaction is correct?

A The atoms are joined together differently in the reactants and product. This means that the total mass of reactants is different from the total mass of product.

B The number of atoms of each element in the reactants is the same as the number in the product. This means that the total mass of reactants is equal to the total mass of product.

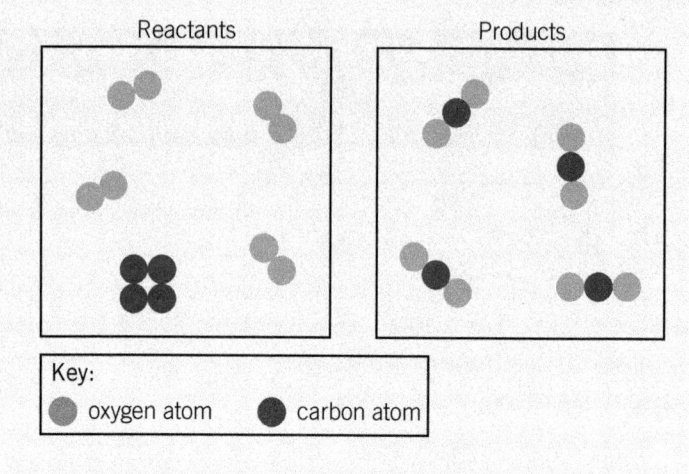

C There are the same number of atoms of each element in the reactants and in the product. This means that the reactants and product have the same properties.

D The product is a gas. This means that the total mass of product is less than the total mass of reactants.

Key:
- oxygen atom
- carbon atom

Follow-up activities

A Look again at the diagram above. Then circle the correct **bold** words and phrases in the sentences below.

There are two reactants, oxygen **gas / solid** and solid carbon. In the diagram, the reactants box shows **four / eight** oxygen atoms and four carbon atoms. The chemical reaction has one product, carbon dioxide. In the diagram, the products box shows **three / four** molecules of carbon dioxide. Each carbon dioxide molecule is made up of one carbon atom joined to **two / three** oxygen atoms. This means that, in the products, there are a total of **four / eight** oxygen atoms and four carbon atoms. The number of oxygen atoms in the reactants is **more than / the same as** the number of oxygen atoms in the product, and the number of carbon atoms in the reactants is **more than / the same as** the number of carbon atoms in the product. Since the mass of each atom is fixed, and there is the same number of atoms of each element in the reactants as in the products, the total mass of reactants is **equal to / more than** the total mass of product.

Hint: The mass of an atom does not change. If there are the same number of atoms of each type before and after a chemical reaction, does the total mass change? For help, see 6.3.1 Atoms in chemical reactions and 6.3.4 Conservation of mass.

B a Calculate the missing masses for the reactions shown in the word equations below.

   i   sulfur   +   oxygen   →   sulfur dioxide
         6.4 g   6.4 g   _____ g

   ii   methane   +   oxygen   →   carbon dioxide   +   water
         1.6 g   6.4 g   _____ g   3.6 g

   iii   calcium carbonate   →   calcium oxide   +   carbon dioxide
           _____ g   5.6 g   4.4 g

b Explain why, for every chemical reaction, the total mass of products is equal to the total mass of reactants. Use ideas about atoms in your answer.

_____

_____

_____

_____

Hint: In a chemical reaction, the atoms are rearranged and joined together differently. Atoms cannot be created or destroyed. For help, see 6.3.1 Atoms in chemical reactions and 6.3.4 Conservation of mass.

C The diagrams show atoms of the reactants and product in the chemical reaction of nitrogen with oxygen.

Key:
● oxygen atom
● nitrogen atom

a Tick the **three** statements about the reactants and products in the chemical reaction that are **true**.

1. There are four nitrogen atoms in the reactants and two nitrogen atoms in the product. ☐
2. There are two oxygen atoms in the reactants and two oxygen atoms in the product. ☐
3. The atoms are joined together in the same way in the reactants and in the products. ☐
4. The properties of a substance depend on what types of atoms are in its particles. ☐
5. The properties of a substance are not influenced by how its atoms are joined together. ☐
6. The reactants and product have different properties. ☐

b Now write corrected versions of the three statements that are **false**.

_____

_____

_____

_____

_____

_____

Hint: The properties of a substance depend on the number and type of atoms of each element in its particles, as well as how the atoms are arranged and joined together. For help, see 6.3.1 Atoms in chemical reactions, 5.3 3 Compounds, and 5.3.4 Chemical formulae.

D The diagram shows how atoms are rearranged when sulfur burns to make sulfur dioxide.

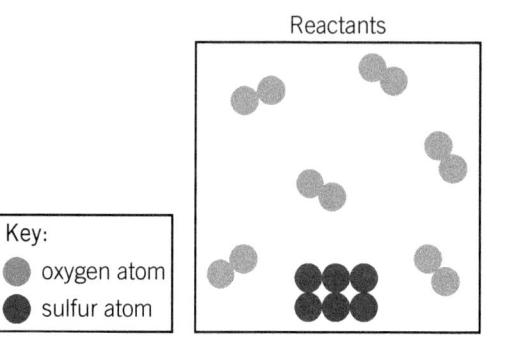

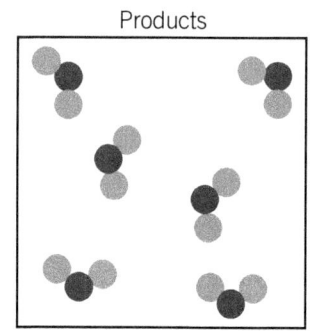

Reactants | Products

Key:
- oxygen atom
- sulfur atom

Write down **eight** correct sentences about the reaction in the diagram using the sentence starters and endings below. Use each starter and ending once, twice, or not at all.

Starters:
- One of the reactants, sulfur,
- One of the reactants, oxygen,
- The product, sulfur dioxide,
- When the chemical reaction occurs,
- The mass of an atom never changes
- The total mass of atoms in the reactants

Endings:
- atoms are rearranged.
- is in the solid state.
- is equal to the total mass of atoms in the product.
- is in the gas state.
- atoms are not destroyed.
- atoms join together differently.
- even when it is in a substance that is in the gas state.

Hint: The same number of atoms of each type are in both the reactants and products of a chemical reaction. Also, a gas has mass. These two facts mean that mass is conserved, even if one or more of the reactants or products is in the gas state. For help, see 6.3.1 Atoms in chemical reactions and 6.3.4 Conservation of mass.

Pinchpoint review

Now look back at the question – do you think you chose the right letter?
Turn to the Answers page to find out.

7.3.1 Global warming

A Draw a line to match each gas to its percentage in the Earth's atmosphere.

Gas	Percentage in Earth's atmosphere
argon	0.04
carbon dioxide	1
nitrogen	21
oxygen	78

Note: The percentages do not add up to 100% owing to rounding.

B Circle the correct **bold** words and phrases in the sentences below.

The transfer of energy from the Sun to the thermal store of gases in the atmosphere is called **global warming / the greenhouse effect**. The gradual increase in the surface temperature of the Earth is called **global warming / the greenhouse effect**. Two greenhouse gases are **methane / nitrogen** and **carbon dioxide / argon**.

C Write the number of one label next to each arrow, to show what each arrow represents.

1. The Earth's surface emits radiation.
2. The Sun warms the Earth's surface.
3. The atmosphere reflects and absorbs some radiation from the Sun.
4. The atmosphere absorbs and radiates some radiation from the Earth's surface.

D Look at the graph.
Tick the statement or statements about the graph that are true.

1. The graph shows that the concentration of carbon dioxide in the atmosphere has increased since 1800. ☐
2. The graph shows that in 1960 the concentration of carbon dioxide was between 310 and 320 parts per million. ☐
3. The graph shows that the global average air temperature has increased since 1960. ☐

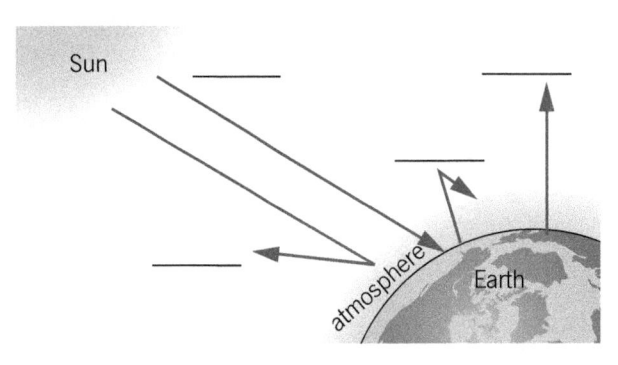

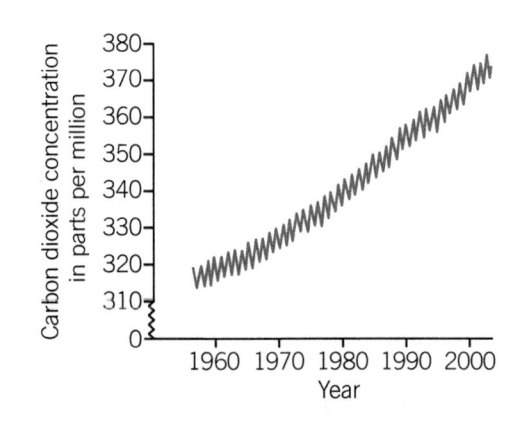

What you need to remember

The air around us is called the _____. The greenhouse effect is when energy from the Sun is _____ to the thermal energy store of gases in the Earth's atmosphere. Greenhouse gases include methane and carbon _____. Global warming is the gradual increase in the air _____ at the surface of the Earth.

65

7.3.2 The carbon cycle

A Highlight or underline the carbon sinks (stores of carbon and its compounds) in the list below.

oceans **fossil fuels** **all igneous rocks**

the atmosphere **solar panels** **some sedimentary rocks**

B Circle the correct **bold** words in the sentences below.

Carbon dioxide is entering and leaving the atmosphere all the time. For many years, carbon dioxide was added to the atmosphere at the same rate as it left the **oceans / atmosphere**. The concentration of carbon dioxide **did not change / increased**. More recently, the concentration of carbon dioxide in the atmosphere has **decreased / increased**. This is because it is added to the atmosphere **faster / slower** than it is removed.

C Colour the processes that **add** carbon dioxide to the atmosphere red.
Colour the processes that **remove** carbon dioxide from the atmosphere green.

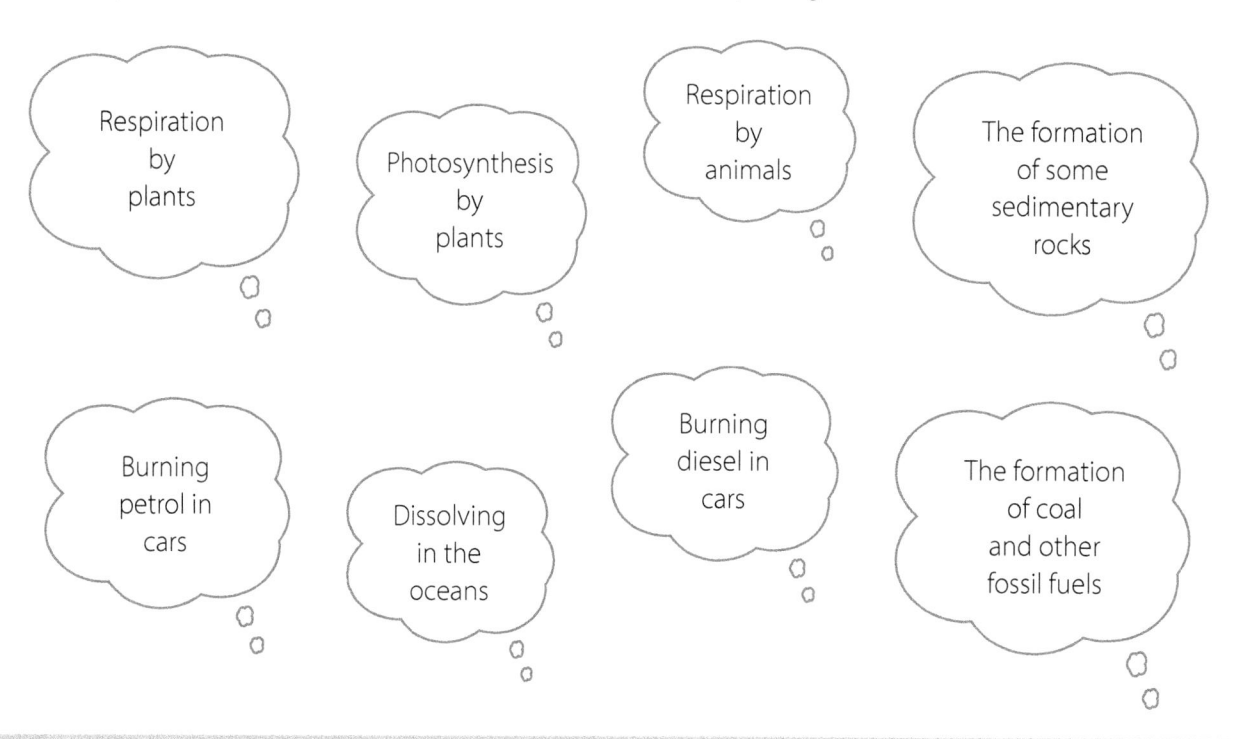

- Respiration by plants
- Photosynthesis by plants
- Respiration by animals
- The formation of some sedimentary rocks
- Burning petrol in cars
- Dissolving in the oceans
- Burning diesel in cars
- The formation of coal and other fossil fuels

What you need to remember

There are several carbon stores, or _____. These include the atmosphere, the ocean, some _____ rocks, _____ fuels, plants and animals, and the soil. The carbon _____ shows how carbon atoms are recycled when they move between stores. For example, carbon dioxide enters the atmosphere when plants and animals _____. It also enters the atmosphere when fossil fuels _____. Carbon dioxide leaves the atmosphere when plants use it in _____. It also leaves the atmosphere by _____ in oceans. Before industrialisation, carbon dioxide was added to the atmosphere at the _____ rate as it left the atmosphere. This meant that the concentration of carbon dioxide did not _____.

7.3.3 Climate change

A Complete the table to match each word or phrase with its definition. Choose from the list below.

| climate change | global warming | greenhouse effect | deforestation |

Word or phrase	Definition
	the gradual increase in the surface temperature of the Earth
	changes to long-term weather patterns
	cutting down or burning forests
	when energy from the Sun is transferred to the thermal energy store of gases in the Earth's atmosphere, keeping the surface of the Earth warmer than it would otherwise be

B Draw a line to match each cause to one direct effect.

Cause
- Deforestation
- Burning fossil fuels
- Every year, more carbon dioxide is added to the atmosphere than is removed
- Climate change

Effect
- More carbon dioxide goes into the atmosphere
- The concentration of carbon dioxide in the atmosphere increases
- Less carbon dioxide is removed from the atmosphere
- Glaciers melt, some plant and animal species become extinct, it is harder for humans in some areas to grow enough food

C Tick the statements below that are evidence that global warming is caused by human activities.
1. Humans have burned increasing amounts of fossil fuels since 1960. ☐
2. Experiments show that burning fossil fuels makes carbon dioxide gas. ☐
3. Scientists have measured the concentration of carbon dioxide in the air since the 1950s. The concentration has greatly increased. ☐
4. When volcanoes erupt, they give out greenhouse gases. ☐
5. Experiments show that carbon dioxide molecules store energy. ☐

What you need to remember

Human activities affect the carbon _____. For example, burning fossil fuels increases the concentration of _____ dioxide in the atmosphere. This extra carbon dioxide causes an increase in the air _____ at the surface of the Earth. This is global _____. Global _____ makes glaciers and polar _____ melt. Global warming also causes climate change, which is a change to long-term _____ patterns. Examples of climate change include more frequent droughts and heatwaves in some areas, and more rainfall in other areas. Climate change leads to some animal and plant _____ becoming extinct and makes it harder for humans to grow enough _____.

7.4.1 Extracting metals

A Most metals are found in the Earth as compounds. A few are found as elements.
Circle the correct **bold** words in the sentences below.

An element is a substance that **can / cannot** be broken down into other substances. All the atoms in an element are **the same / different**. A compound is a substance made up of atoms of two or **more / fewer** elements. The atoms of the different elements in a compound are **not / strongly** joined together.

B The box shows part of the reactivity series.
  a Circle the name of the **non-metal** element in the reactivity series.
  b In the list below, circle the names of the metals that can be extracted from their compounds by heating with the non-metal from part **a**.

  aluminium   copper   iron   lead   magnesium   zinc

  c Explain your answer to part **b**.
  _____
  _____

sodium
magnesium
aluminium
carbon
zinc
iron
lead
copper

C a Explain why aluminium is extracted from its compounds by electrolysis. Use the reactivity series in activity **B** to help you.
  _____
  _____

  b When a mining company finds an aluminium ore deposit, the manager must decide whether it is worth mining the ore and extracting aluminium from it. Below is a list of quantities the manager must take into account.
  Draw an upwards arrow ↑ next to quantities that, if they have high values, will support a decision to mine the ore.
  Draw a downwards arrow ↓ next to quantities that, if they have low values, will support a decision to mine the ore.

  1 The percentage of aluminium in the ore. ☐
  2 The mass of waste produced when 1 kg of aluminium oxide is separated from the ore. ☐
  3 The distance from the mine to a place where electrolysis can take place. ☐
  4 The cost of electricity. ☐
  5 The mass of greenhouse gases made when the electricity is generated. ☐
  6 The price the aluminium can be sold for. ☐

What you need to remember

Most metals exist in the Earth's _____ as compounds. These compounds are _____ with other compounds in rock. A rock that it is worth extracting a metal from is called an _____.

Metals that are _____ carbon in the reactivity series can be extracted from their compounds by heating with carbon. Metals that are above carbon in the reactivity series are extracted from their compounds by _____.

7.4.2 Recycling

A Tick the statements below that are true.
1. There is only a limited amount of gold on Earth, so the slower gold is extracted, the sooner it will run out. ☐
2. Recycling tin reduces the need to mine more tin ore. ☐
3. The more energy that is required to extract 1 kg of a metal from its ore, the more important it is to recycle that metal. ☐

B The statements below can be reordered to describe how aluminium is recycled. Read the statements and write down the order of statements you think will give the best description.

Correct order ☐ ☐ ☐ ☐ ☐

1. Use a lorry to collect used cans.
2. Pour the liquid aluminium into a mould.
3. Leave the liquid aluminium to cool and freeze.
4. Melt the shreds of aluminium in a furnace.
5. Shred the cans.

C Aluminium may be obtained from its ore, or by recycling used aluminium objects. Tick one box next to each statement to show whether the statement is describing an advantage or a disadvantage of recycling.

	Statement	✓ if this is an advantage of recycling	✓ if this is a disadvantage of recycling
1	Recycling uses less energy.		
2	Some people do not like sorting their waste.		
3	The world's aluminium ore will last longer.		
4	Recycling reduces the need to extract resources.		
5	The lorries that collect cans for recycling use diesel as a fuel.		

D Different plastics must be sorted before recycling. If a plastic is less dense than water, it floats. If a plastic is more dense than water, it sinks. The bar chart shows the densities of four plastics. The density of water is 1.0 g/cm^3.

  a Explain how these 4 plastics can be partly separated using water.

  _____

  _____

  b Explain why the data in this question must be displayed on a bar chart, not a line graph.

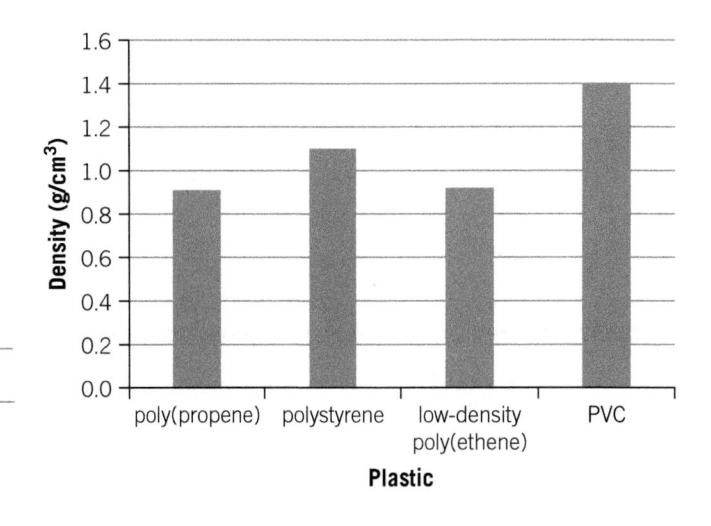

  _____

What you need to remember

Recycling means collecting and _____ used materials so that they can be used again. There are many advantages of recycling, including _____ the need to extract resources.

69

Big Idea 7 Pinchpoint

Pinchpoint question

Answer the question below, then do the follow-up activity **with the same letter** as the answer you picked.

The diagram represents the carbon cycle. Each numbered arrow represents a process that moves carbon dioxide into or out of the atmosphere.

Which statement about the carbon cycle is correct?

A The greenhouse effect only occurs if processes 2 and 3 occur faster than processes 1 and 4.

B Global warming occurs if processes 2 and 3 occur very fast.

C Global warming occurs if processes 2 and 3 occur faster than processes 1 and 4.

D Global warming occurs if processes 1 and 2 occur faster than processes 3 and 4.

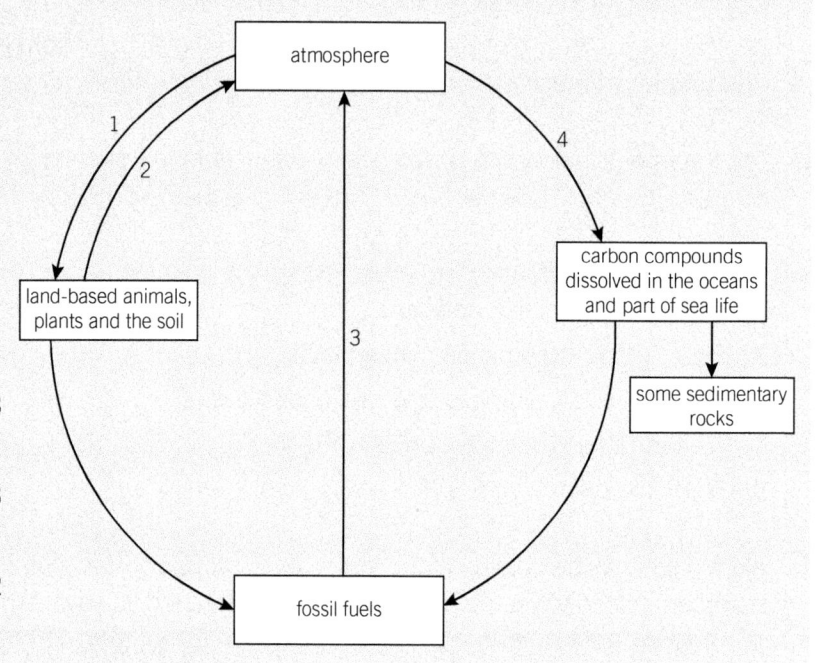

Follow-up activities

A Draw a line to match each phrase to its definition.

climate change	when energy from the Sun is transferred to the thermal energy store of gases in the Earth's atmosphere, keeping the surface of the Earth warmer than it would otherwise be
global warming	a substance that contributes to the greenhouse effect, such as carbon dioxide
greenhouse effect	changes to long-term weather patterns
greenhouse gas	the gradual increase in the average surface temperature of the Earth

Hint: Global warming and the greenhouse effect are not the same thing. For help, see 7.3.1 Global warming, 7.3.2 The carbon cycle, and 7.3.3 Climate change.

B Tick the statements below that are true.
1 Process 1 is respiration. ☐
2 Process 2 is photosynthesis. ☐
3 Process 3 is combustion. ☐
4 Process 4 is dissolving. ☐
5 Processes 1 and 3 add carbon dioxide to the atmosphere. ☐
6 Processes 2 and 4 remove carbon dioxide from the atmosphere. ☐

7 Whether or not global warming occurs depends on two factors: how quickly carbon dioxide is added to the atmosphere, and how quickly it is removed. ☐

8 If carbon dioxide is added to the atmosphere faster than it is removed, global warming occurs. ☐

Hint: The amount of carbon dioxide in the atmosphere depends on how quickly it is added to the atmosphere **and** on how quickly it is removed. For help, see 7.3.1 Global warming and 7.3.2 The carbon cycle.

C a Complete the table by writing one word from the list in each box.

| combustion | dissolving | photosynthesis | respiration |

Arrow number	Name of process
1	
2	
3	
4	

b Explain how humans have contributed to global warming, particularly since the 1960s.

_____

_____

Hint: To answer part **b**, think about human activities that add carbon dioxide to the atmosphere. For help, see 7.3.1 Global warming and 7.3.2 The carbon cycle.

D Circle the correct **bold** words and phrases in the sentences below.

Carbon **sinks / taps** absorb and store carbon and its compounds. Carbon sinks include the atmosphere, some **igneous / sedimentary** rocks, and fossil fuels. The carbon **cycle / square** shows how carbon and its compounds enter and leave carbon sinks.

The **photosynthesis / respiration** of plants and animals produces carbon dioxide, which is added to the atmosphere. The **combustion / formation** of fossil fuels also adds carbon dioxide to the atmosphere. Two processes remove carbon dioxide from the atmosphere – **photosynthesis / respiration** by plants, and dissolving in the ocean.

If carbon dioxide is added to the atmosphere **faster / slower** than it is removed, the amount of carbon dioxide in the atmosphere increases. This causes global warming.

Hint: If the amount of carbon dioxide in the atmosphere increases, global warming occurs. For help, see 7.3.1 Global warming and 7.3.2 The carbon cycle.

Pinchpoint review

Now look back at the question – do you think you chose the right letter?
Turn to the Answers page to find out.

Section 2 Revision questions

1. Which gas is present in the largest amount in the Earth's atmosphere? Tick **one** box. *(1 mark)*

   argon ☐   carbon dioxide ☐

   nitrogen ☐   oxygen ☐

2. What are the starting substances called in **every** chemical reaction?

   Tick **one** box. *(1 mark)*

   elements ☐   reactants ☐

   products ☐   compounds ☐

3. Which statements about chemical reactions are **always** true?

   Tick **two** statements. *(2 marks)*

   New substances are made. ☐

   Energy is transferred to the surroundings. ☐

   Atoms are rearranged and join together differently. ☐

   The products are compounds. ☐

4. Mrs Allfrey adds a small piece of sodium to a large amount of water. She observes vigorous bubbling.

   What are the products of the reaction?
   Tick **two** boxes. *(2 marks)*

   hydrogen ☐   oxygen ☐

   sodium chloride ☐   sodium hydroxide ☐

5. **Table 1** shows properties for three elements in the same group of the Periodic Table. The elements are in the same order in the Periodic Table.

   Table 1

Element	Density (g/cm³)	Melting point (°C)
Manganese	7	1240
Technetium	11	2200
Rhenium	21	3180

   a. Plot the **density** data on a bar chart. Use the following axes. *(1 mark)*

   b. Describe the pattern in the **melting point** data in **Table 1**. *(1 mark)*

   _____

   _____

6. **Table 2** shows some properties of three polymers.

   Table 2

Polymer	Properties
Low-density poly(ethene)	• flexible • absorbs some liquids
Nylon 6.6	• absorbs water • reacts with sulfuric acid
Poly(propene)	• stiff and rigid • does not absorb water • does not react with acids or solvents

   Write down the name of **one** polymer from the table that can be used to make fuel tanks for cars. *(1 mark)*

   _____

7. A teacher mixes two elements – aluminium and iodine. He adds a drop of water, and the students see bright white flames. In the chemical reaction, the elements make a compound, aluminium iodide. A student writes down some of his observations in **Table 3**.

   Table 3

Substance	Appearance
aluminium	shiny silver-coloured powder
iodine	grey crystals
aluminium iodide	white powder

   a. What is the chemical symbol of aluminium?
   Tick **one** box. *(1 mark)*

   AL ☐   al ☐   aL ☐   Al ☐

b Define the term 'element'. *(2 marks)*

c Write down one conclusion that the student could make about elements and compounds from the information in **Table 3**. *(1 mark)*

8 The diagrams show molecules of some elements and compounds. Draw a line from each diagram to the correct formula. *(4 marks)*

Key:
- nitrogen atom
- oxygen atom

Formulas: NO₂, NO, N₂, N₂O, O₃

9 **Figures 1** and **2** show particle diagrams for two reactions.

Figure 1

Figure 2

Key:
- hydrogen atom
- oxygen atom
- nitrogen atom

a Explain why **Figure 1** shows a combustion reaction. *(1 mark)*

b Name the type of reaction shown in **Figure 2**. *(1 mark)*

c Complete the table below for the reaction shown in **Figure 1**. *(1 mark)*

Stage of reaction	Number of nitrogen atoms shown in the reactants	Number of oxygen atoms shown in the products
Before the reaction		
After the reaction		

d Use information from the table to explain how **Figure 1** demonstrates that atoms are conserved in a chemical reaction. *(1 mark)*

10 A compound has the formula SiO₂.

a Write down the number of oxygen atoms that are in the compound for every one silicon atom. *(1 mark)*

b Write down the number of oxygen atoms that are in the compound for every 10 silicon atoms. *(1 mark)*

11 Substance **X** has the formula O₂. Substance **Y** has the formula SO₂.
Compare substances **X** and **Y** in terms of:
- type of substance
- number of atoms. *(4 marks)*

12 Here are four word equations.

W magnesium + oxygen → magnesium oxide

X ice → liquid water

Y magnesium carbonate → magnesium oxide + carbon dioxide

Z hydrogen peroxide → water + oxygen

a Write down the letter of the **one** equation that shows a change of state. *(1 mark)*

_____

b Write down the letter of the **one** equation that shows two elements joining together. *(1 mark)*

_____

c Write down the letters of **two** equations that show decomposition reactions. *(2 marks)*

_____ and _____

d Write down the letter of the **one** equation that shows an exothermic reaction. *(1 mark)*

_____

e Write down the letter of the **one** equation that shows a combustion reaction. *(1 mark)*

_____

13 A teacher heats up some iron. She places it in a jar of bromine gas. The reacting mixture of iron and bromine glows bright red.

At the end, there is a brown powder in the jar. This is iron bromide.

The word equation for the reaction is:

iron + bromine → iron bromide

a Describe one piece of evidence that shows there is a chemical reaction. *(1 mark)*

_____

b The teacher started with 1 g of iron. The mass of iron bromide at the end was 5.3 g. Calculate the mass of bromine that reacted with the iron.

Show how you worked out your answer. *(2 marks)*

_____

mass of bromine = _____ g

14 Explain how burning increasing amounts of fossil fuels causes flooding in areas near the sea. *(6 marks)*

_____
_____
_____
_____
_____
_____

15 The box shows part of the reactivity series of metals. It includes one non-metal, carbon.

| lithium |
| magnesium |
| aluminium |
| carbon |
| iron |
| tin |
| lead |

a Suggest whether lithium is extracted from its minerals by heating with carbon, or by electrolysis. Justify your answer. *(1 mark)*

_____
_____

b Suggest **two** other metals in the reactivity series above that are extracted from their minerals in a similar way to lithium. *(1 mark)*

_____ and _____

c Justify your answer to part **b**. *(1 mark)*

_____
_____

16 Hydrogen reacts with fluorine to make hydrogen fluoride.

Figure 3 shows how the atoms are rearranged in the chemical reaction.

Key:
○ hydrogen atom
● fluorine atom

Figure 3

a Name the **two** substances in which bonds break in the chemical reaction. *(1 mark)*

_____ and _____

b Name the **one** substance in which a new bond is made in the chemical reaction. *(1 mark)*

_____

c In this reaction, the energy needed for bond breaking is less than the energy released on bond making. Identify whether the reaction is endothermic or exothermic and explain your answer. *(2 marks)*

_____
_____

Section 2 Checklist

Revision question	Outcome	Topic reference	☹	😐	🙂
1	State the names and percentages of the gases that make up the Earth's atmosphere.	7.3.1			
2	State that the starting substances in a chemical reaction are called reactants.	6.3.1			
3	State that in a chemical reaction atoms are rearranged, but the total number of atoms is conserved.	6.3.1			
4	State that the elements in Group 1 all react with water to make hydrogen gas and the metal hydroxide.	5.4.2			
5a	Add data to a graph or chart.	EP3			
5b	Use data to describe a trend in physical properties.	5.4.1			
6	Explain how polymer properties make them suitable for their uses.	5.3.5			
7a	Write down chemical symbols correctly.	5.3.1			
7b	State what an element is.	5.3.1, 5.3.3			
7c	Compare the properties of a compound to the properties of the elements whose atoms it contains.	5.3.3			
8	Represent elements, compounds and mixtures using particle diagrams.	5.3.4			
9a	Interpret particle diagrams to explain what happens in a chemical reaction.	6.3.1			
9b	Interpret a particle diagram to identify a combustion reaction.	6.3.2			
9c, d	Interpret a particle diagram to identify the atoms in the reactants and products of a chemical reaction.	6.3.1			
10a, b	Interpret chemical formulae.	5.3.4			
11	Compare formulae of an element and a compound.	5.3.4			
12a	Interpret word equations to identify a change of state.	6.3.1			
12b	Interpret word equations to identify a reaction in which two elements join together to make one compound.	6.3.1			
12c	Interpret word equations to identify a decomposition reaction.	6.3.3			
12d	Interpret word equations to identify an exothermic reaction. Recognise that combustion reactions are exothermic.	6.3.2 6.4.1			
12e	Interpret word equations to identify a combustion reaction.	6.3.2			
13a	Identify evidence for chemical reactions.	6.3.1			
13b	Given data and a word equation, calculate reacting masses.	6.3.4			
14	Explain how global warming causes flooding in coastal areas.	7.3.3			
15a	Justify the choice of extraction method for a metal, given data about reactivity.	7.4.1			
15b	Suggest metals that are extracted by electrolysis.	7.4.1			
15c	Justify the choice of extraction method for a metal, given data about reactivity.	7.4.1			
16a	State that, in chemical reactions, bonds in reactants are broken.	6.4.3			
16b	State that, in chemical reactions, new bonds are made.	6.4.3			
16c	Use ideas about bond energies to explain energy changes in chemical reactions.	7.4.3			

8.3.1 Gas exchange

A Use the words in the box below to label the diagram of the human respiratory system.

| alveoli | bronchi | bronchiole | diaphragm | lungs | rib | trachea |

5 _____
1 _____
2 _____
3 _____
4 _____
6 _____
7 _____

B There are millions of alveoli in the lungs. Tick the box(es) below to show how alveoli are able to exchange gases quickly and easily.

Alveoli walls are only one cell thick. ☐   Alveoli create a large surface area. ☐

Alveoli walls are strong and thick. ☐   Alveoli have a poor blood supply. ☐

C These pie charts show the difference in composition of inhaled and exhaled air. Use the data to complete the table below, using the terms **more**, **less**, or **same**.

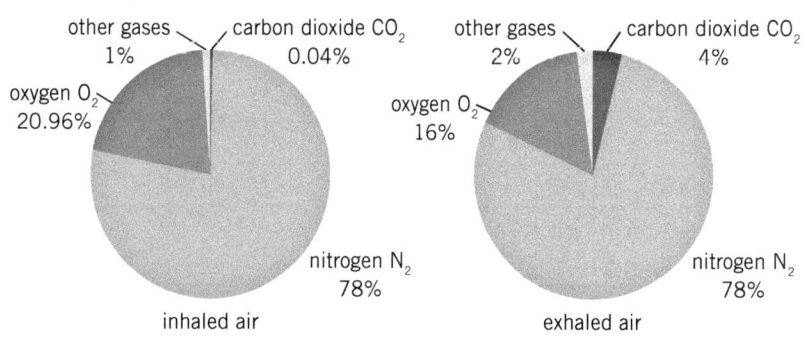

inhaled air: other gases 1%, carbon dioxide CO_2 0.04%, oxygen O_2 20.96%, nitrogen N_2 78%

exhaled air: other gases 2%, carbon dioxide CO_2 4%, oxygen O_2 16%, nitrogen N_2 78%

Gas	Inhaled air	Exhaled air
carbon dioxide		
nitrogen		
oxygen		

What you need to remember

Breathing is carried out by the _____ system and the major organs of this system are your _____. You inhale in order to take in _____ from the air and _____ in order to remove carbon dioxide. When you inhale, air travels in through your mouth and nose and then through your _____. It then travels into your lungs through the _____ and then through a bronchiole, finally moving into an air sac called an _____. These have thin walls and create a large surface area for _____, which means that the gases can diffuse in and out of the blood easily.

8.3.2 Breathing

A A bell jar model can be used to model what happens during breathing. Add the following labels to the diagram of a bell jar model, to show what each part represents.

| diaphragm | lung | chest cavity | trachea |

- tube _____
- bell jar _____
- balloon _____
- rubber _____

B Circle the correct **bold** words in the sentences below to describe what happens when you **inhale**.

The muscles between your ribs **contract / relax** – this pulls your ribcage **down and in / up and out**.
The diaphragm **contracts / relaxes** – it moves **down / up**.
The volume inside your chest cavity **increases / decreases**.
The pressure inside your chest cavity **increases / decreases**.
This draws air **into / out of** the lungs.

C The statements below can be reordered to explain how you can measure your lung volume. Write down the order of statements you think will give the best method.

Correct order ☐ ☐ ☐ ☐ ☐ ☐

1. Calculate the difference in the water levels – this is your lung volume.
2. Turn the bottle of water upside down in a tank of water.
3. Read the new level of water in the bottle.
4. Read the level of water in the bottle.
5. Take a deep breath, then breathe out for as long as possible into the tube.
6. Fill a plastic bottle full of water and place a plastic tube in the neck of bottle.

What you need to remember

When you inhale, the muscles between your _____ and your diaphragm _____. This _____ the volume of your chest cavity which _____ the pressure, causing air to be drawn in. When you exhale, the muscles _____; this _____ the volume of your chest cavity. This _____ the pressure and forces air _____. You can use a _____ to model this process. Smoking and diseases such as _____ can reduce lung _____.

8.3.3 Drugs

A Drugs are chemicals which affect the way your body works.
Sort the following list of drugs into those which are medicinal and those which are recreational.

| ecstasy | caffeine | antibiotic | alcohol | paracetamol | tobacco | ibuprofen |

Medicinal	Recreational

B Circle **medicinal** or **recreational** for the following statements about drugs.

1. They have health benefits. — **medicinal / recreational**
2. They are taken for enjoyment. — **medicinal / recreational**
3. Many are illegal. — **medicinal / recreational**
4. They are prescribed by a doctor. — **medicinal / recreational**

C Draw a line to match each recreational drug with its effect on health.

alcohol	speeds up the nervous system
tobacco	significantly increases risk of lung cancer and heart disease
caffeine	slows down the nervous system and damages the liver

D **a** Describe what is meant by a drug addinction.

_____

_____

b Name **two** withdrawal symptoms a person with a drug addiction may experience if they try to stop taking a drug.

1 _____

2 _____

What you need to remember

Chemicals that affect the way your body works are called _____. _____ drugs are taken for enjoyment, whereas _____ drugs benefit your health. If you regularly take a drug, you may develop an _____. If you then try to stop taking the drug, you may suffer from unpleasant _____ _____, which make it harder to give up.

8.3.4 Alcohol

A Drinking alcohol has several effects on the body.
Write these effects in the correct box on the diagram opposite:

unconsciousness

feeling relaxed and happy

difficulty walking and talking (drunk)

death

no alcohol

INCREASING INTAKE

excessive alcohol

How a person would be affected

B Tick the **two** organs in your body alcohol is most likely to damage.

Lungs ☐   Liver ☐

Brain ☐   Heart ☐

C Circle the correct **bold** words in the sentences below about alcohol.

Alcohol contains the drug **caffeine / ethanol**. This is absorbed into your **lungs / bloodstream**, and then travels to the brain affecting your **nervous / digestive** system. It is called a **stimulant / depressant** because it **slows down / speeds up** your reactions.

D Circle **true** or **false** for the following statements about alcohol and pregnancy. Drinking alcohol…

1. increases the risk of miscarriage — **true / false**
2. reduces the birth weight of babies — **true / false**
3. increases the amount of sperm produced — **true / false**
4. can damage the foetus's brain, causing learning difficulties — **true / false**

What you need to remember

Alcoholic drinks contain the drug _____. This acts on the _____ system and slows down body reactions; it is called a _____. Drinking too much alcohol can result in _____ and brain damage. Different alcoholic drinks contain different amounts of alcohol. 10 ml of alcohol is known as one _____ of alcohol. The government recommends that adults drink less than 2–3 units a day to remain healthy. People who are addicted to alcohol are known as _____.

79

8.3.5 Smoking

A Smoking increases your chances of developing many diseases.

Circle **three** diseases people are more likely to develop if they smoke.

| diabetes | lung cancer | heart attack | AIDS | stroke | measles |

B Choose which of the following components of tobacco smoke are being described in the sentences below. You can use each word more than once.

| tar | carbon monoxide | nicotine |

Stimulant which speeds up the nervous system: _____

Sticky black material that collects in lungs: _____

Addictive chemical: _____

Contains chemicals which can cause cancer: _____

Gas which stops blood from carrying as much oxygen as it should: _____

C Tick **two** boxes to show the risks of smoking in pregnancy:

Baby being obese ☐

Low birth weight baby ☐

Miscarriage during pregnancy ☐

Baby suffering from Down's syndrome ☐

D Smoking causes diseases that affect the lungs and circulatory system.

Describe how smoking causes the following.

a Emphysema _____

_____

b Heart disease _____

_____

What you need to remember

Smoking increases the risk of many conditions such as lung _____ and _____ attacks. The risk of someone else developing one of these conditions also increases if they breathe in the smoke. This is called _____ smoking. Tobacco smoke contains many harmful chemicals such as tar which narrows the _____, carbon _____ which reduces the amount of _____ the blood can carry, and nicotine. As well as being addictive nicotine is a _____ which makes the heart beat faster. Smoking in pregnancy affects foetal development and can cause _____.

8.4.1 Nutrients

A From the list below, circle the **nutrients** your body needs.

| lipid   oxygen   blood   protein   vitamin   bread   carbohydrate |

B Choose **one** food type from the box below to complete each row of the table.

| fruit   pasta   fish   butter |

Good source of ……..	Food
Protein	
Vitamins and minerals	
Carbohydrate	
Lipid	

C Draw a line to match each nutrient with its role in the body.

carbohydrate		growth and repair of body tissues
lipid		main source of energy
protein		needed in all cells and body fluids
water		store of energy, keep you warm, protect organs
vitamin		needed in tiny amounts to keep you healthy

D Circle **true** or **false** for the following statements about dietary fibre.

1. It is a nutrient.   **true / false**
2. It adds bulk to help keep food moving through gut.   **true / false**
3. It helps prevent constipation.   **true / false**
4. It is found in animal products like milk.   **true / false**

What you need to remember

To remain healthy you must eat a _____ diet. This means eating food containing the right _____ in the right amounts. These include _____ and _____ which give you energy, _____ for growth and repair, _____ and _____ to keep you healthy, and water and dietary _____ to keep the food moving through your gut.

81

8.4.2 Food tests

A Many food tests involve adding a solution to the food sample.
Tick the change below that is used to show which nutrients the food contains.

The solution evaporates ☐

The solution freezes ☐

The solution changes colour ☐

A gas is given off ☐

B The following pieces of equipment are used in food tests.

| water bath   pestle and mortar   filter paper   pipette |

Complete the table to match the piece of equipment with its use.

Equipment	Use
	Grind up food into small pieces
	Transfer small amounts of liquid
	Remove solid material from solution
	Heat solution to a specific temperature

C Circle the correct **bold** words in the sentences below to describe one way you can test for lipids in a solid piece of food.

Rub some food onto a piece of **filter paper / cardboard**.

Hold the paper **under running water / to the light**.

If the paper **goes translucent / turns blue** it contains lipids.

D You can test foods to find out what food molecules they contain.

Draw lines to connect the food being tested to the chemical used and the result if the molecule is present

Food molecule	**Chemical to use**	**Result if food being tested contains the molecule**
starch	ethanol	blue-black colour
sugar	blue Benedict's solution	purple colour
protein	orange iodine solution	cloudy, white layer
lipid	blue copper sulfate and sodium hydroxide solution	brick-red colour

What you need to remember

Scientists use _____ to find out which nutrients are present in a food product.
_____ turns blue-black when _____ is present. Benedict's solution turns orange-_____ if sugar is present. A solution of copper sulfate and sodium hydroxide solution will turn _____ if _____ is present. Ethanol will turn _____ if lipids are present.

8.4.3 Unhealthy diet

A Circle the correct **bold** words in the sentences below.

Your body needs **energy / light** to function properly.

The energy contained in food is measured in **grams / joules**.

The amount of energy everybody needs is the **same / different**.

The more exercise you do, the **more / less** energy your body requires.

B The following people need different amounts of energy each day. Put them in order, from those who need the least to the most energy.

Correct order ☐ ☐ ☐ ☐

1 adult male builder
2 female teenager
3 5-year-old child
4 adult male IT technician

C If you are malnourished, you are eating the wrong amount or wrong type of food. Draw a line to match each health issue with its dietary cause.

Obesity	Eating foods lacking in vitamins or minerals
Deficiency	Eating too much food or too many fatty foods
Starvation	Eating too little food

D The list shows some symptoms of an unbalanced diet. Sort the symptoms into the correct column to show whether they are more likely to occur in a person who is obese or underweight.

lack of energy   diabetes   heart disease   poor immune system

Obese	Underweight

What you need to remember

Eating the wrong amount or wrong types of food is called _____. If the energy in the food you eat is less than the energy you use, you will lose body mass and become _____. You are also likely not to take in the correct amount of a vitamin or mineral. This is called a _____ and can make you ill. Not eating enough food for prolonged periods is called _____.

If you take in more energy than you use by eating too much, you will gain body mass as _____, which is stored under the skin. Extremely overweight people are said to be _____.

8.4.4 Digestive system

A Circle the correct **bold** words in the sentences below to describe what happens during digestion.

During digestion, **large / small** molecules such as proteins are **broken down / joined together** into **large / small** molecules.

B Label the diagram of the digestive system using the key terms from the box below.

| stomach | rectum | small intestine | gullet | large intestine |

mouth (containing teeth, tongue, and salivary glands)

liver

pancreas

anus

C Complete the table below to show the different parts of the digestive system, using the key words in the box.

| stomach | anus | small intestine | gullet | large intestine |

Digestive system organ	What happens there
	nutrient molecules are absorbed into blood
	undigested food (faeces) leaves the body
	food is mixed with digestive juices and acids
	muscular tube that squeezes food from the mouth into the stomach
	water passes into body and faeces form

What you need to remember

The group of organs which work together to break down food is called the _____. Food enters the mouth and travels down your _____ into your _____. Here it is mixed with _____ and digestive juices. As a result of _____, small molecules of nutrients are produced which pass through the _____ intestine into the blood. Water passes back into the body in the _____ intestine leaving undigested food called faeces. This is stored in the _____ until it leaves the body through the _____.

8.4.5 Bacteria and enzymes in digestion

A Enzymes are involved in digestion. Circle the enzymes in the list below.

| bile | bacteria | protease | carbohydrase | glycerol | probiotic | lipase |

B Where in your digestive system do helpful gut bacteria make vitamins?

Mouth ☐

Stomach ☐

Small intestine ☐

Large intestine ☐

C Circle **true** or **false** for the following statements about enzymes.

1. They are made of lipids. — **true / false**
2. They speed up digestion. — **true / false**
3. They are known as biological catalysts. — **true / false**
4. They are used up during a reaction. — **true / false**

D Each type of enzyme is involved in a different reaction.
Draw a line to match each type of enzyme to the molecule it breaks down and the molecules that are produced.

Enzyme	Molecule it breaks down	Molecules produced
Carbohydrase	Lipid	Sugars
Protease	Carbohydrate	Fatty acids and glycerol
Lipase	Protein	Amino acids

What you need to remember

Some gut _____ living in your large intestine help you to remain healthy by making _____.
Special proteins called _____ help speed up digestion without being used up. They are a type of _____. There are three main types – _____ which breaks down carbohydrate molecules into _____ molecules, _____ which breaks down _____ into amino acids and _____ which breaks down lipid molecules into fatty acids and _____.
To help further with lipid digestion, _____ breaks the lipids into smaller droplets that are easier for the enzymes to work on.

Big Idea 8 Pinchpoint

Pinchpoint question

Answer the question below, then do the follow-up activity **with the same letter** as the answer you picked.

Digestion begins in your mouth.

Read the statements below and choose which one correctly describes the action of the enzymes present in saliva.

- **A** The enzymes live in cells and speed up a reaction before being used up.
- **B** The enzymes break down carbohydrates into amino acids.
- **C** Saliva contains protease enzymes which break down protein molecules.
- **D** The enzymes break down carbohydrate molecules into sugar molecules.

Follow-up activities

A Write down **four** correct sentences about enzymes using the sentence starters and endings below. You should use one starter twice to make the fourth sentence.

| Enzymes are catalysts. This means they… |
| Enzymes are made of… |
| Enzymes are not living as they cannot… |

| …are not used up in a reaction. |
| …respire. |
| …speed up a reaction. |
| …protein molecules. |

Hint: Remember all living organisms have to be able to perform MRS GREN. For help, see 8.4.5 Bacteria and enzymes in digestion.

B Complete the diagrams below to show how the enzymes break large molecules down into smaller molecules during digestion. Fill in all the missing names for the reactants, enzymes, and products.

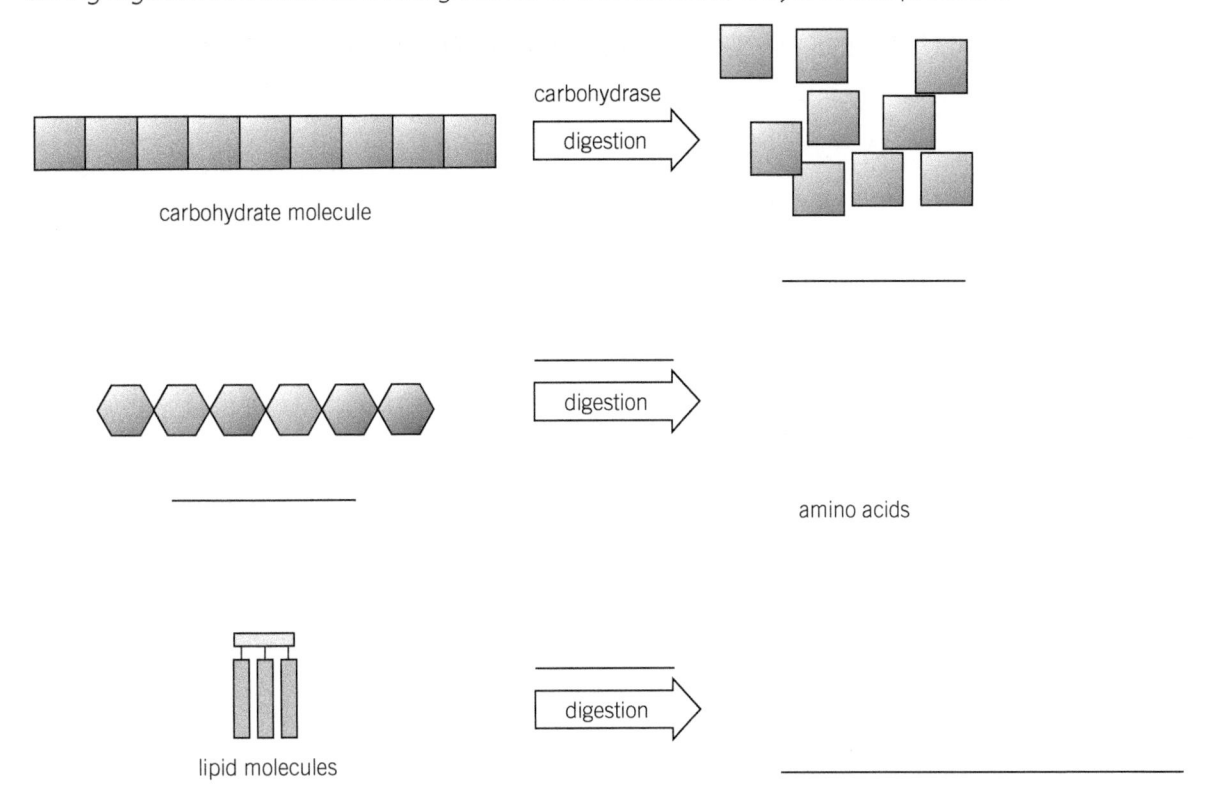

carbohydrate molecule → carbohydrase digestion → _____

_____ → digestion → amino acids

lipid molecules → digestion → _____

Hint: Look at the start of each enzyme's name. It gives you a clue to what it breaks down. For help, see 8.4.5 Bacteria and enzymes in digestion.

C a Complete the following table to show where enzymes are found in the body. Add a tick for each place the enzyme is found.

Enzyme	Mouth	Stomach	Small intestine
Carbohydrase			
Protease			
Lipase			

b Complete the following sentences using the words in the box below.

| stomach   lipase   lipids   carbohydrase   lipids |
| protease   mouth   protein   carbohydrate |

Bread can be broken down in the _____. This is because it contains lots of the nutrient _____ which is broken down by a _____ enzyme.

Butter cannot be broken down until it reaches the _____. This is because butter contains lots of _____. These are broken down by a _____ enzyme.

Fish is rich in _____. These large molecules are broken down into smaller molecules by a _____ enzyme.

Hint: There is only one type of enzyme found in the mouth. It breaks down large carbohydrate molecules into sugars. For help, see 8.4.5 Bacteria and enzymes in digestion.

D There are two main types of washing powder: biological and non-biological powders. Biological washing powders contain enzymes as well as detergents; non-biological powders do not contain enzymes.

Explain why enzymes are added to washing powder to help get clothes clean. Include a specific example to help in your explanation.

Hint: Think about the cause of many of the 'dirty' marks on clothes. For help, see 8.4.5 Bacteria and enzymes in digestion.

Pinchpoint review
Now look back at the question – do you think you chose the right letter?
Turn to the Answers page to find out.

9.3.1 Aerobic respiration

A Tick the box which names the process where energy is released in cells.

Photosynthesis ☐   Respiration ☐

Chemosynthesis ☐   Digestion ☐

B Complete the word equation for aerobic respiration using words from the box below.

| oxygen   water   light   carbon dioxide   starch |

glucose + _____ ⟶ water + _____ (+ energy)

C Name the **two** reactants needed for aerobic respiration.

1 _____

2 _____

D Aerobic respiration takes place in one part of the cell.
On the diagram of an animal cell below, label this part with its name.

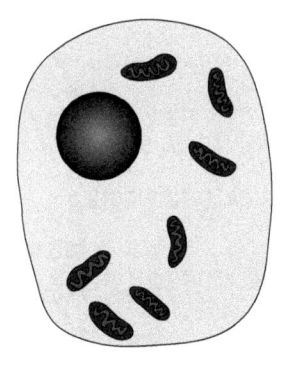

What you need to remember

Energy is released in your cells by _____ _____. During this process, _____ and oxygen react inside your _____ to release energy. The waste products carbon dioxide and _____ are also produced.

Glucose is produced when _____ are broken down during digestion. Glucose is transported around your body in the _____ in the blood.

Oxygen is also transported by the blood. It binds to the _____ in red blood cells.

89

9.3.2 Anaerobic respiration

A Which of the following word equations correctly shows anaerobic respiration in animal cells?

glucose → lactic acid + carbon dioxide ☐

glucose → lactic acid ☐

glucose → ethanol + carbon dioxide ☐

glucose → water + carbon dioxide ☐

B Describe a situation where a person may use anaerobic respiration.

_____

C The table shows some statements about respiration.
Tick **one** column in each row to show which statements are true for each type of respiration.

	✓ if true for aerobic respiration	✓ if true for anaerobic respiration
Glucose is a reactant		
Oxygen is a reactant		
Carbon dioxide is produced		
Lactic acid is produced		
Water is produced		
Transfers more energy per glucose molecule		

D Circle **true** or **false** for the following statements about anaerobic respiration.
1 Lactic acid produced can cause muscle cramp. **true / false**
2 Carbon dioxide is used to break down lactic acid. **true / false**
3 When yeast respires anaerobically, it produces lactic acid. **true / false**
4 The word equation for fermentation is:
glucose → ethanol + carbon dioxide (+ energy) **true / false**

What you need to remember

When your body respires without oxygen it is called _____. This produces _____ which can build up in your muscles and cause cramp. To break down the acid, you have to breathe in extra oxygen. This is called an _____.
Microorganisms such as yeast carry out a type of anaerobic respiration called _____. In this reaction, carbon dioxide and _____ are produced.

9.3.3 Biotechnology

A In biotechnology, organisms are used to make useful products.

Tick the organism below that is used when bread is made.

Bacteria ☐

Yeast ☐

Virus ☐

Mushroom ☐

B Bread is made using the chemical reaction fermentation.

Circle **true** or **false** for the following statements about fermentation.

1. Reaction needs oxygen — **true / false**
2. It is a type of anaerobic respiration — **true / false**
3. Reaction produces lactic acid — **true / false**
4. Reaction produces ethanol — **true / false**

C Complete the word equation for fermentation.

Choose from the following words:

| ethanol | oxygen | lactic acid | glucose | water |

_____ → _____ + carbon dioxide

D The statements below can be reordered to describe how beer and wine are made.
Read the statements and write down the order that you think will give the best description.

Correct order ☐ ☐ ☐ ☐ ☐

1. The liquid is put into bottles or barrels
2. The mixture is left until all the sugar has fermented
3. Yeast is added to plant sugar in a large container
4. The yeast ferments the sugar into alcohol
5. The liquid is filtered to remove any sediment

What you need to remember

The microorganism _____ is used to make bread and alcoholic drinks such as _____ and wine. During _____, glucose is converted into carbon dioxide and _____.
_____ in yeast speed up this process making the reaction occur _____.

9.4.1 Photosynthesis

A Plants make their own food through the process of photosynthesis. Tick where photosynthesis takes place.

Nucleus ☐

Cytoplasm ☐

Chloroplast ☐

Mitochondria ☐

B Tick the **two** products of photosynthesis.

Glucose ☐

Fat ☐

Oxygen ☐

Carbon dioxide ☐

C Use the words below to complete the word equation for photosynthesis.

| oxygen | water | light |

Carbon dioxide + _____ ⟶ glucose + _____

(above arrow: _____)

D Draw a line to match each substance needed in photosynthesis with how it enters the plant.

Carbon dioxide		Absorbed by chlorophyll in chloroplasts
Water		Enters through tiny holes on the underside of the leaf
Light		Diffuses into root hair cells

What you need to remember

Plants and _____ are called _____ because they make their own food by the process of _____. Animals are called _____ as they have to eat other organisms to survive. During photosynthesis, carbon dioxide and _____ are converted into oxygen and _____ using energy from the Sun. This light energy is absorbed by _____ in chloroplasts.

9.4.2 Leaves

A Label the diagram of the cross-section through a leaf using the key words in the box below.

| waxy layer | palisade layer | spongy layer | chloroplast |
| air space | stoma | guard cell |

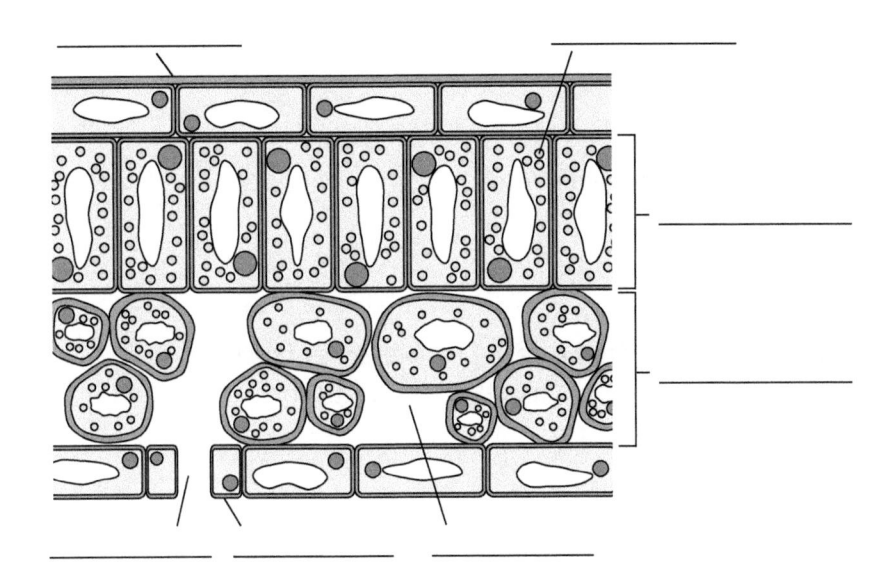

B Draw a line to match each main component in a leaf with its function.

Chloroplast	Open and close stomata
Stomata	Contains chlorophyll to trap sunlight
Guard cells	Transport water to cells in leaf
Veins	Allow gases to diffuse into and out of leaf
Waxy layer	Reduces water loss through evaporation

C Circle **true** or **false** for the following statements about the palisade layer.

1. Found at the bottom of the leaf — true / false
2. Main site of photosynthesis — true / false
3. Contains many air spaces — true / false
4. Contains cells packed with chloroplasts — true / false

What you need to remember

Photosynthesis in a plant mainly takes place in the _____, though a small amount occurs in the stems. The underneath of a leaf contains tiny holes called _____ which allow _____ to diffuse into the leaf and _____ to diffuse out. Water is carried to the leaf in the _____. Most photosynthesis occurs in the cells of the _____ layer as most light reaches this layer. Therefore, these cells are full of _____.

9.4.3 Investigating photosynthesis

A Which of the following techniques can be used to measure the rate of photosynthesis of pondweed? Tick **one** box.

Number of bubbles given off in a set time ☐

Colour change ☐

Decrease in mass ☐

B Name **two** factors that affect the rate at which a plant photosynthesises.

1 _____

2 _____

C The statements below can be reordered to describe how to test a leaf for the presence of starch. Read the statements and write down the order that you think will give the best description.

Correct order ☐ ☐ ☐ ☐ ☐

1 Add a few drops of iodine solution
2 Iodine will turn blue-black if starch is present
3 Wash leaf and place on white tile
4 Place leaf in boiling water
5 Place in boiling ethanol to remove chlorophyll

D The following sentences describe how temperature, light intensity, and concentration of carbon dioxide affect the rate of photosynthesis. Circle the correct **bold** words in the sentences below to complete the sentences.

The higher the light intensity, the **slower / faster** the rate of photosynthesis.

The lower the concentration of carbon dioxide, the **slower / faster** the rate of photosynthesis.

The higher the temperature, the **slower / faster** the rate of photosynthesis. However, if the temperature is too hot,

the enzymes **start / stop** working and photosynthesis **starts / stops**.

What you need to remember

You can test a leaf for starch by adding a few drops of _____. It will change from yellow-orange to _____-_____. You can measure how fast a plant is photosynthesising by counting the number of bubbles of _____ given off in a fixed time.

The main factors which affect the rate of photosynthesis are _____ intensity, _____ _____ concentration, and _____. In general, increasing each of these factors _____ the rate of photosynthesis.

9.4.4 Plant minerals

A To remain healthy, plants need to take in minerals. Circle the minerals in the list below.

| water | nitrates | glucose | oxygen | potassium |

B To ensure plants have enough minerals and do not suffer from a deficiency, some farmers add man-made chemicals to the soil plants are growing in. Tick the chemicals added.

Anti-fungals ☐

NPK fertilisers ☐

Manure ☐

Compost ☐

C Draw a line to match each mineral to its use in the plant, and describe the plant's appearance if this mineral is deficient.

Mineral	Function	Deficiency symptoms
Nitrate	Making chlorophyll	
Phosphate	Healthy growth	
Potassium	Healthy roots	
Magnesium	Healthy leaves and flowers	

D Circle the correct **bold** words in the sentences below to explain how nitrates are taken in by plants and involved in growth.

Plants get the minerals they need from the **air / soil**. The minerals are dissolved in the **air / soil**. Minerals are absorbed by the plant's **stomata / root hair cells** and are then transported around the plant by the **phloem / xylem**. Nitrates are involved in making **amino acids / sugars**. These join together to form **carbohydrates / proteins**.

What you need to remember

To stay healthy, plants need to absorb _____ from the soil. For healthy growth, plants need four minerals – _____ to make chlorophyll, _____ for healthy leaves and flowers, _____ for healthy growth and _____ for healthy roots. If a plant does not get enough of a mineral it is said to have a _____ and will not grow properly. To prevent this occurring, farmers add chemicals called _____ to the soil.

Big Idea 9 Pinchpoint

Pinchpoint question

Answer the question below, then do the follow-up activity **with the same letter** as the answer you picked.

Which of the following statements best describes the process of aerobic respiration?

A It is represented by the word equation: carbon dioxide + water → glucose + oxygen (+ energy)

B A process that occurs in only animal cells to transfer energy for movement.

C A chemical reaction where glucose reacts with oxygen to release energy and other waste products.

D Taking in oxygen through your lungs and releasing carbon dioxide.

Follow-up activities

A The following sentences describe what happens in aerobic respiration.
Read the sentences then complete the activities below.

Your body needs energy for everything it does.

You get your energy from organic molecules in the food you eat.

To release the energy stored in food, glucose reacts with oxygen in a reaction called aerobic respiration.

This transfers energy to your cells.

As a result of the reaction, carbon dioxide and water are produced.

a Underline the **two** reactants of aerobic respiration.

b Circle the **two** waste products of aerobic respiration.

c Complete the word equation for respiration.

_____ + _____ ⟶ _____ + _____

Hint: Reactants are the starting substances in a chemical reaction. For help, see 9.3.1 Aerobic respiration.

B a Complete the following table using the terms **yes**, **no**, or **yes – some species** to show what types of chemical reaction occur in each of the following organisms.

Organism	Aerobic respiration	Photosynthesis
Animal		
Plant		
Microorganism		

b Complete the following sentences.

All living organisms r_____ to transfer energy from glucose. This can be used for m_____ and g_____.

Green organisms, such as p_____ and some b_____, are able to p_____ to transfer light energy. This is used to produce g_____ molecules for the organism.

Hint: Remember all living organisms have to be able to perform MRS GREN. Can you remember what each letter in this mnemonic stands for? For help, see 9.4.1 Photosynthesis and 9.3.1 Aerobic respiration.

C The energy released during respiration supplies all the energy needed for living processes in a cell. Explain why the following cells need energy:

   a Muscle cell

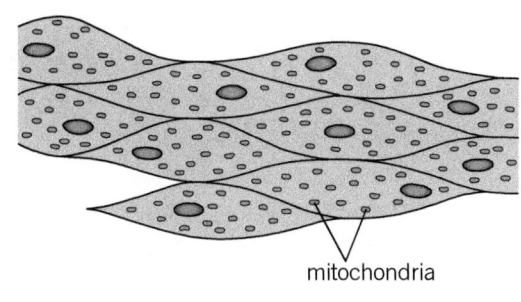

   _____

   _____

   _____

   _____

   _____

   b Sperm cell

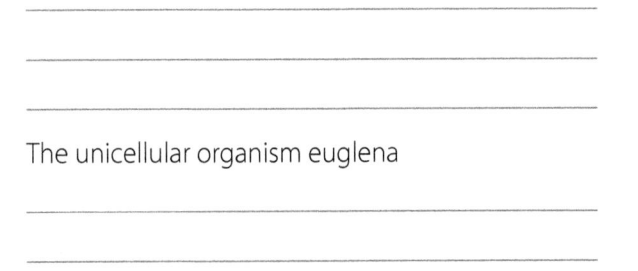

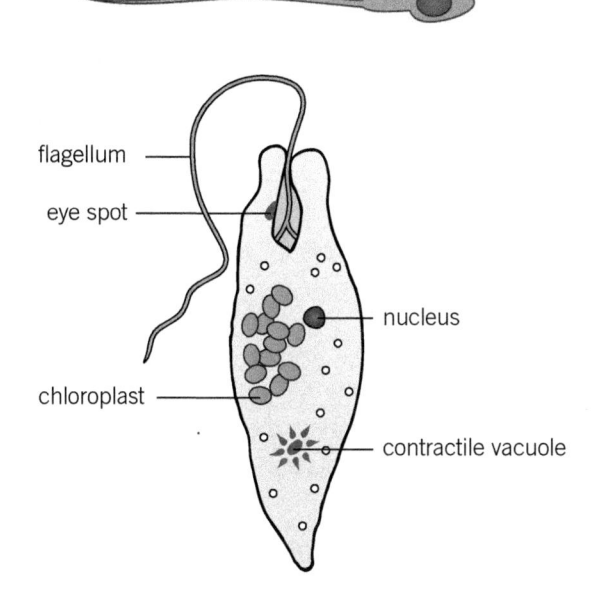

   _____

   _____

   _____

   _____

   c The unicellular organism euglena

   _____

   _____

   _____

   _____

Hint: Think about the main function of each cell. For help, see 9.3.1 Aerobic respiration and 8.2.5 Uni-cellular organisms.

D Circle the correct **bold** terms in the sentences below to describe how the substances needed for respiration enter the body, and the waste products produced leave the body.

Glycerol / glucose is a carbohydrate found in food. These small molecules are released during **digestion / photosynthesis**.

Glucose molecules are absorbed by the wall of the **large / small** intestine and pass into your blood.

Glucose **diffuses / dissolves** into the cells that need it for respiration.

Oxygen is taken into your lungs when you **inhale / exhale**. This is also known as **breathing / respiration**.

It diffuses into your blood through the **amoeba / alveoli** and is carried to the cells which need it for respiration.

Carbon dioxide / nitrogen is produced as a result of respiration. If this builds up in the body it can cause harm.

Carbon dioxide diffuses into the blood and is carried to the lungs where it is **inhaled / exhaled**.

Hint: You breathe to allow gas exchange to take place in the lungs. Where does respiration occur in the body? For help, see 9.3.1 Aerobic respiration.

> **Pinchpoint review**
> Now look back at the question – do you think you chose the right letter?
> Turn to the Answers page to find out.

10.3.1 Natural selection

A Which of the following statements describes evolution? Tick **one** box.

Differences in characteristics within a species. ☐

When no more individuals of a species are left anywhere in the world. ☐

Changes in species over time. ☐

B The peppered moth is often used to study evolution. Circle the correct **bold** words in the sentences below to describe how this species has evolved.

There are two types of peppered moth: pale moths and dark moths. Before the industrial revolution there were more **pale / dark** moths as these were **camouflaged / highlighted** against the pale tree bark. This is because **pale / dark** moths were seen and eaten. More **pale / dark** moths survived and reproduced, **increasing / decreasing** the number of pale moths in the population.

After the industrial revolution, many trees were covered in soot. The **pale / dark** moths were now more camouflaged, so they survived and reproduced, and more **pale / dark** moths were eaten. This resulted in the number of pale moths **increasing / decreasing** and the number of dark moths **increasing / decreasing**. Most moths in the population were then **pale / dark**, as these survived and reproduced.

C The statements below can be reordered to describe how a species evolves through the process of natural selection. Read the statements and write down the order of statements you think will give the best description.

Correct order ☐ ☐ ☐ ☐ ☐ ☐

1 Process is repeated over many generations.
2 Genes which code for advantageous characteristics are passed on to offspring.
3 New species can evolve where all organisms have the adaptations.
4 Organisms in a species show variation.
5 More organisms within the species have the advantageous characteristic.
6 The organisms with the characteristics that are best suited to the environment survive and reproduce. Less well-adapted organisms die.

D What **two** types of physical evidence do we have for evolution?

1 _____
2 _____

What you need to remember

All organisms living today have _____ from a common ancestor. This process has taken _____ of years and has occurred as a result of _____.

The organisms most adapted to their environment _____ and reproduce, passing on the _____ which code for these characteristics to their offspring. The remains of organisms that lived millions of years ago, called _____, provide evidence for evolution.

10.3.2 Charles Darwin

A Tick the box of the process that natural selection leads to.

Extinction ☐

Selective breeding ☐

Evolution ☐

Captive breeding ☐

B Before scientists publish their work in a scientific journal, it is peer-reviewed

Circle the correct **bold** words in the sentences below about peer review.

Darwin developed his theory of evolution following observations on organisms in the **Galapagos / Greek** islands.

At the same time another scientist called **Crick / Wallace** was working on his own theory of natural selection and evolution. He gathered his evidence from South America and Asia.

The two scientists read and **evaluated / understood** each other's work. This is called peer review.

Their ideas were so similar that they jointly **reviewed / published** the theory of evolution in a scientific paper.

C Draw lines to match the evidence to how it supports Darwin's theory of natural selection.

Fossil record	Micro-organisms best suited for their environment survive and reproduce
Finch beak and claws	Organisms have changed over time (millions of years)
Extinction	Birds best suited to available food survive and reproduce. Eventually all birds on the island have same characteristics
Development of antibiotic-resistant bacteria	Species that do not adapt to environmental changes die out

---

What you need to remember

Charles _____'s theory states that organisms _____ as a result of natural _____. He noticed that finches on different islands in the Galapagos had different _____ and claws.

These were linked to the type of food available. He concluded that if a bird was born with a beak suited to the food available it would survive and _____. Over time, all the birds on this island would have this characteristic.

Before he published this theory, it was _____ reviewed by a fellow scientist called Alfred _____.

10.3.3 Extinction

A Match the definitions with the words in the box below.

| biodiversity | extinct | endangered |

The variety of organisms living in an area: _____.

Species of plants and animals that only have a small population in the world: _____.

No individuals of a species living anywhere in the world: _____.

B Which of the following organisms are examples of animals that are now extinct?
Tick as many answers as you need.

Elephant ☐

Ammonite ☐

Dinosaur ☐

Penguin ☐

C Draw a line to match each factor with how it could lead to the extinction of a species.

Outbreak of disease	Whole population eaten before they have the chance to reproduce successfully
Prolonged drought	Lack of food and/or water causing death of whole population
Introduction of new predators	Whole population killed by a microorganism
Introduction of new competitors	Loss of food source or shelter leads to death of whole population
Deforestation	Lack of water leads to death of whole population

D Circle the correct **bold** words in the sentences below about biodiversity.

Having **many / a few** different species present within an ecosystem ensures that resources are available for other populations.

A woodland has **high / low** biodiversity. If one species of tree is destroyed there will be **no / many** others available for food or **light / shelter**. This means other populations of organisms will **survive / die**.

A desert has **high / low** biodiversity. If one species of plant is destroyed, there **may / may not** be another for populations of other organisms to feed on. So other species will **survive / die**.

What you need to remember

The range of organisms living in area is called _____. Destruction of _____ and outbreaks of _____ can cause a reduction in biodiversity and can lead to a species becoming _____. This is where there are no individuals of a species living anywhere in the world. When only a small number of a species exist, the species is said to be _____.

10.3.4 Preserving biodiversity

A The following definition can be used to describe an extinct species:

> When no more individuals of a species remain anywhere in the world.

Rewrite this definition for an endangered species.

_____

_____

B Which of the following techniques do scientists use to try to protect endangered species?

Tick as many answers as you need.

Gene banks ☐

Poaching ☐

Captive breeding ☐

Habitat removal ☐

C Draw a line to match each method of preventing extinction with its description and how it works.

| Conservation | Breeding animals in human-controlled environments | Increases organisms' chance of survival and reduces disruption to food chains |

| Captive breeding | Protecting a natural environment | Creates a healthy stable population that can be reintroduced back into the wild |

D Circle the correct **bold** words in the sentences below about gene banks.

Gene banks store **genetic / live** samples of different species.

They are normally stored at very **high / low** temperatures.

They can be used for research and to create new **individuals / species**.

What you need to remember

Species that are risk of becoming extinct are said to be _____. Scientists use a number of techniques to prevent this occurring. This includes protecting habitats through _____, the _____ breeding of animals, and storing genetic samples in gene _____. Preserving biodiversity not only ensures that a species _____ but can provide useful resources for other organisms, including humans.

10.4.1 Inheritance

A Complete the following sentences about DNA, genes, and chromosomes using the words in the box below.

| DNA | genes | chromosomes |

Your genetic information is stored on a long molecule called _____ which is packaged into long strands called _____. Small sections of these molecules are called _____ and contain the information to produce a characteristic.

B Match each label on the diagram to the correct word below.
Write **S**, **T**, **U**, or **V** beside each word.

gene ☐

chromosome ☐

cell ☐

nucleus ☐

C You inherit characteristics from your parents through genetic material.
Circle the correct **bold** words in the sentences below to describe how genetic material is inherited.

Inside the nucleus of your cells, DNA is arranged into long strands called **genes / chromosomes**. You inherit **half / all** your chromosomes from your mother and **half / all** your chromosomes from your father. Chromosomes from your mother are carried in **an egg / a sperm** cell. Chromosomes from your father are carried in **an egg / a sperm** cell. During **variation / fertilisation**, the nuclei of the two cells join, producing an embryo with a full set of **23 / 46** chromosomes.

What you need to remember

You inherit characteristics from your parents through genetic material found in the _____ of your cells. Genetic material is made up of the chemical _____ – this contains all the information needed to make an organism. In the nucleus, this chemical is organised into long strands called _____. Each strand is divided into sections called _____. Each section contains the information needed to produce a characteristic.

10.4.2 DNA

A The scientists James Watson and Francis Crick were involved in discovering the structure of DNA. Choose the **two** other scientists involved from the list below.

Charles Darwin ☐

Maurice Wilkins ☐

Rosalind Franklin ☐

Joseph Lister ☐

B Circle the correct **bold** words in the sentences below to describe the structure of DNA

DNA is made up of **two / three** strands.

The strands are twisted together to form a double **helix / ladder** shape.

The strands are joined together by **two / four** different chemical **acids / bases**.

Everyone's DNA is different, except for **siblings / identical twins**.

C Choose from the words below to fill in the blanks in the sentences.

sharing	pea	helix	structure	working
nucleus	discoveries		DNA	characteristics

The earliest work on how _____ are inherited was completed by Gregor Mendel, in 1866. He experimented on _____ plants. A few years later, Friedrich Meischer discovered an acidic substance in the _____ of cells. We now call this substance DNA.

By the early 1950s, Maurice Wilkins and Rosalind Franklin used X-rays to photograph crystals of _____.

This work enabled James Watson and Francis Crick to work out the _____ of the DNA molecule. They deduced it has a double _____ shape.

The discovery of the structure of DNA is the result of many scientists _____ together, through _____ their results. This is the way many scientific _____ are made.

What you need to remember

Your DNA is found in the _____ of your cells. It is made of _____ strands. These are twisted together to form a double _____. The strands are held together by four different _____.

The structure of DNA was discovered by four scientists. Wilkins and _____ took a picture of DNA using _____. _____ and Crick looked at this image and identified that the structure of DNA was a _____ shape.

103

10.4.3 Genetics

A Draw a line to match each key term with its definition.

allele	Version of the gene always expressed if present
dominant allele	Different forms of the same gene
recessive allele	Two copies are needed to be expressed in the organism

B In humans, freckles are a dominant characteristic. This dominant allele can be represented using F. The recessive allele is represented by f.

Circle whether a person will have freckles or not with the following allele combinations:

FF	**freckles / no freckles**

Ff	**freckles / no freckles**

ff	**freckles / no freckles**

C In mice, black fur is dominant (D) and white fur is recessive (d).

Complete the following Punnett square to show the likelihood of a mouse having black fur.

The female mouse carries alleles DD; the male mouse carries alleles dd.

	Female	
	D	D
Male d		
d		

_____ of the offspring will have black fur

D Use the Punnett square below to show what would happen if you cross two mice with the alleles Dd.

	Female	
Male		

_____ % of mice will have black fur

_____ % of mice will have white fur

What you need to remember

Different forms of the same gene are called _____. If a _____ allele is present it will always be expressed. A _____ allele will only be expressed if two copies of the allele are present.

A _____ square can be used to predict the outcomes of a genetic cross.

10.4.4 Genetic modification

A Circle the correct **bold** words in the sentence below to describe what is meant by genetic modification.

Scientists are now able to alter an organism's **genes / brain** to produce an organism with **unwanted / desired** characteristics.

B Tick the boxes of examples of desired characteristics of genetically modified organisms.

1. frost resistant ☐
2. produce medical drugs ☐
3. low yield ☐
4. produce poisons to kill crop plants ☐

C Reorder the statements below to describe how an organism can be genetically modified.

Correct order ☐ ☐ ☐ ☐

1. Take genes from an organism with that characteristic.
2. As the organism develops, it will display the characteristics of the foreign genes.
3. Identify the desired characteristic such as frost-resistance.
4. Place them into an organism at a very early stage of development.

D Read the statements about the advantages and disadvantages of genetic modification. Write whether each statement is true or false.

Genetically modified products trigger allergic reactions in some individuals. _____

Useful vaccines and antibiotics can be produced. _____

It takes many generations to produce a genetically modified organism. _____

There are ethical concerns over genetic modification. _____

What you need to remember

Scientists can create an organism with desired _____ by taking _____ from another organism. These are called _____ genes. They are placed into plant or animal _____ at a very early stage in development. As the organism develops it will now display the desired characteristics.

Big Idea 10 Pinchpoint

Pinchpoint question

Answer the question below, then do the follow-up activity **with the same letter** as the answer you picked.

Gregor Mendel was one of the first scientists to study inheritance. He studied the inheritance of different characteristics in pea plants.

In one experiment, he crossed red-flowered pea plants with white-flowered pea plants. He found out that the allele for red flowers is dominant (R), and the allele for white flowers is recessive (r).

Calculate how many of the offspring will have white flowers if two plants with the alleles Rr are crossed.

A   1 in 3 plants have white flowers

B   As a ratio of 3 white : 1 red

C   50% of plants are white-flowered

D   ¼ of the plants are white-flowered

Follow-up activities

A Scientists display the possible outcomes from a genetic cross as the probability of a characteristic being expressed. This can be stated in a number of different ways. The table below displays the results you are likely to achieve.

Complete the table.

Probability	Ratio	Percentage	Fraction
4 in 4	4:0		1 or 4/4
3 in 4		75%	¾
2 in 4 (or 1 in 2)	2:2 (or 1:1)	50%	
	1:3	25%	¼

Hint: When working out a ratio, the total number of combinations available (4 in this case) should be the sum of the values in the ratio. For example, a 1:3 ratio means for every 4 possible outcomes, 1 is of one type, while 3 are of the other. For help, see 10.4.3 Genetics.

B Circle the correct **bold** words to complete the following sentences.

Different versions of the same gene are called **chromosomes / alleles**.

A **dominant / recessive** allele is always expressed if it is present.

One copy / two copies of this allele **is / are** needed for a characteristic to be displayed.

A **dominant / recessive** allele is not always expressed if it is present.

One copy / two copies of this allele **is / are** needed for a characteristic to be displayed.

Hint: If a dominant allele is present (this is represented by a capital letter), the organism will always display this characteristic. For help, see 10.4.3 Genetics.

C In another experiment, Mendel crossed pea plants which have green seed pods with pea plants that have yellow seed pods. He found out that the allele for green seed pods is dominant (G), and the allele for yellow seed pods is recessive (g).

    a Use the Punnett square below to help you perform a genetic cross between the two pea plants with the alleles Gg.

		Plant 1	
		G	g
Plant 2	G		
	g		

    b Complete the sentences below.

_____ of the offspring will have the alleles GG and will have _____ flowers

_____ of the offspring will have the alleles Gg and will have _____ flowers

_____ of the offspring will have the alleles gg and will have _____ flowers

Hint: Start by combining the alleles in the table by putting the alleles in the column and row together. For help, see 10.4.3 Genetics.

D Cystic fibrosis is an inherited disorder. It affects cell membranes, causing thick and sticky mucus to be produced. This causes breathing difficulties. Cystic fibrosis is caused by a recessive allele represented by c. The dominant healthy allele is represented by C.

Calculate the likelihood of a mother (Cc) and a father (Cc) having a child with cystic fibrosis.

_____ of the offspring will have cystic fibrosis.

Hint: Begin by drawing a Punnett square so you can work out the possible offspring. For help, see 10.4.3 Genetics.

Pinchpoint review

Now look back at the question – do you think you chose the right letter?
Turn to the Answers page to find out.

Section 3 Revision questions

1. Choose **one** drug from the box below to answer each of the following questions. (You can use each drug more than once.)

caffeine	paracetamol	tobacco
ethanol (alcohol)		antibiotic

   a An example of a recreational drug. *(1 mark)*

   _____

   b An example of a medicinal drug. *(1 mark)*

   _____

   c A drug that can cause lung cancer. *(1 mark)*

   _____

   d A drug that slows down body reactions. *(1 mark)*

   _____

2. Complete the following sentences using words from the box below. *(5 marks)*

genes	nucleus	characteristic
DNA		chromosomes

   Your genetic information is stored in the chemical _____ found in the _____ of your cells. This chemical is arranged into long strands called _____. Small sections of these structures are called _____. Each one contains the information needed to produce a _____.

3. Circle the most appropriate **bold** words to describe what happens when you inhale.

   Your ribs move **down and inwards / up and outwards**. *(1 mark)*

   At the same time, your diaphragm moves **upwards / downwards**. *(1 mark)*

   This **increases / decreases** the pressure in your chest. *(1 mark)*

   Therefore air rushes **inwards / outwards**. *(1 mark)*

4. **Figure 1** shows the human digestive system.

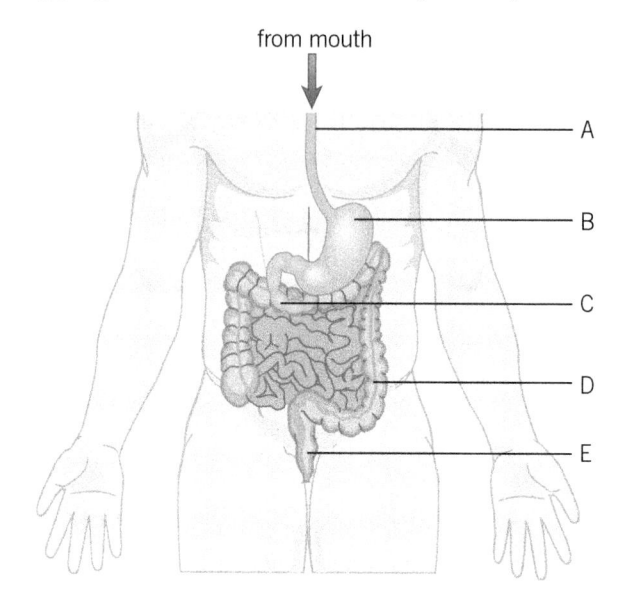

   Figure 1

   a Identify which label on the diagram is pointing to the following structures.

   Stomach _____ *(1 mark)*

   Gullet _____ *(1 mark)*

   Large intestine _____ *(1 mark)*

   b Describe what happens during digestion. *(2 marks)*

   _____
   _____
   _____

5. To remain healthy, you should eat a balanced diet.

   a Name two nutrients that form part of a balanced diet. *(2 marks)*

   _____
   _____

   b Name one health problem a person may have if they eat too much fat. *(1 mark)*

   _____

   c Name one health problem a person may have if they do not eat enough food. *(1 mark)*

   _____

6 Plants make their own food by the process of photosynthesis.

a Give **two** products of photosynthesis. (*2 marks*)

_____

_____

b Name where photosynthesis occurs in a cell. (*1 mark*)

_____

c Plants store glucose in their leaves as starch. **Figures 2** and **3** show two of the main stages used when testing a leaf for starch. Describe the purpose of each step.

i (*2 marks*)

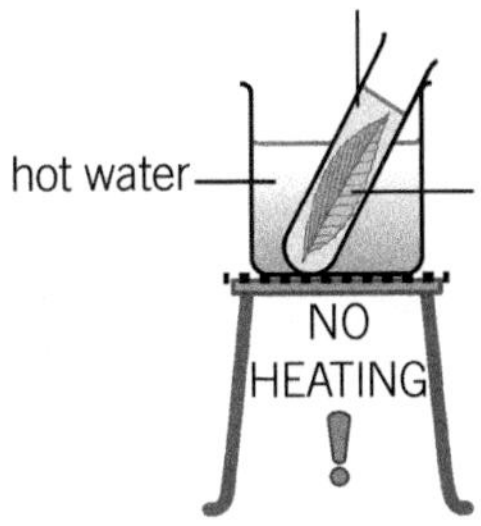

Figure 2

_____

_____

_____

ii (*2 marks*)

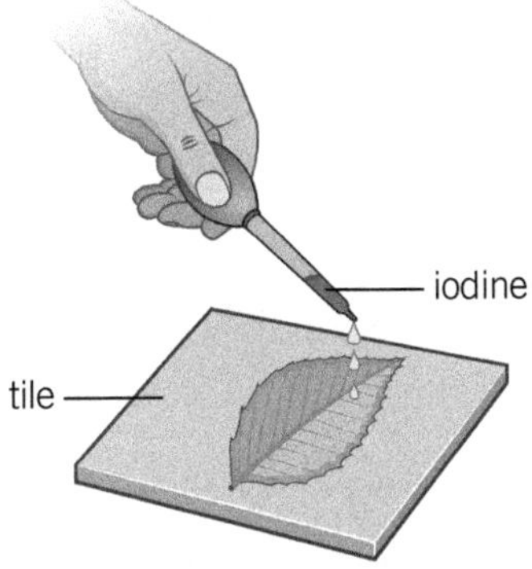

Figure 3

_____

_____

_____

d Explain why the Bunsen burner must be turned off before the step shown in **Figure 2**. (*1 mark*)

_____

7 **Figure 4** shows a structure found in your lungs

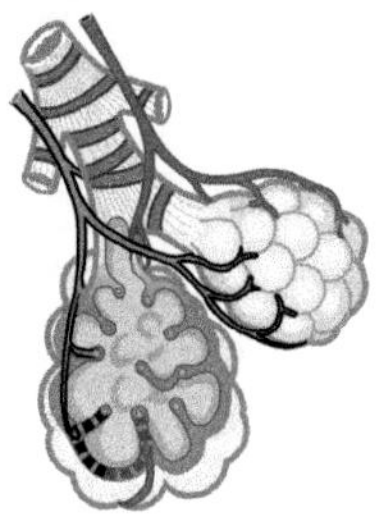

Figure 4

a Name the structure that forms the gas exchange surface. (*1 mark*)

_____

b Describe this structure's role in gas exchange. (*2 marks*)

_____

_____

c Explain how this structure is adapted to perform its function. (*3 marks*)

_____

_____

_____

_____

8 A student measured his lung volume using the equipment shown in **Figure 5**.

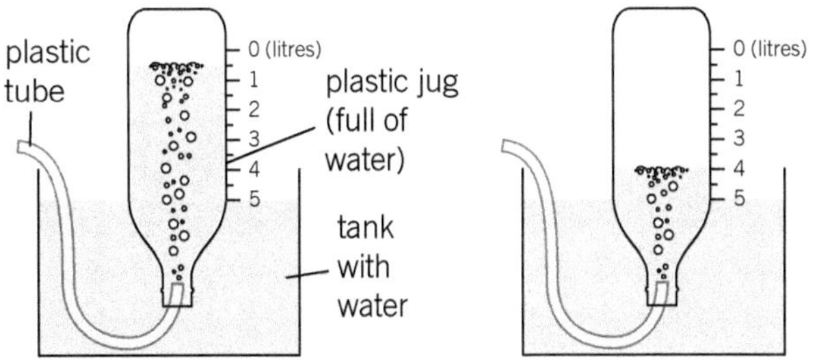

Figure 5

a Calculate the volume of air exhaled by the student. (*2 marks*)

_____ litres

109

b Write down **two** differences between the air exhaled by the student, and the air inhaled. *(2 marks)*

1 _____

2 _____

c Suggest **one** factor that could reduce the student's lung volume. *(1 mark)*

_____

9 A group of students were investigating the types of nutrient present in different ready meals.

a Draw a line to match each nutrient to its role in the body. *(2 marks)*

Protein	Main source of energy
Lipids	To provide a store of energy and insulation, and protect organs
Carbohydrates	To repair body tissues and make new cells

b The ready meals also contained fibre. Explain the importance of fibre in a person's diet. *(2 marks)*

_____
_____
_____

c One of the ready meals stated that it contained 2520 kJ of energy per pack. An average adult requires 8400 kJ of energy per day. Calculate the percentage of an adult's daily energy requirement contained within this pack. *(2 marks)*

_____ kJ

d Describe how the students could prove that sugar was present in one of the ready meals *(3 marks)*

_____
_____
_____
_____

10 Digestion begins in your mouth when food is chewed and mixed with saliva.

a i Name the enzyme present in saliva. *(1 mark)*

_____

ii Describe the role of this enzyme in digestion. *(2 marks)*

_____
_____
_____

b Explain why enzymes are called biological catalysts. *(2 marks)*

_____
_____
_____

c Bacteria that live in your large intestine play an important role in digestion. Describe the role these bacteria play. *(2 marks)*

_____
_____
_____

11 You get energy from the food you eat. This energy is transferred to your cells by respiration.

a i Complete the word equation for aerobic respiration. *(2 marks)*

glucose + _____ →

carbon dioxide + _____

ii Write down where in the cell respiration takes place. *(1 mark)*

_____

b Write down **two** differences between aerobic and anaerobic respiration in humans. *(2 marks)*

_____
_____
_____

c i Write down what type of respiration is being represented by the following word equation:

glucose → ethanol + carbon dioxide (+ energy)
(1 mark)

ii Name an organism that performs this type of respiration. *(1 mark)*

12 Plants and animals compete for resources to survive.

A new predator is introduced into an area. Describe how its prey species could change over a long period of time to survive a new predator. *(6 marks)*

13 a Describe the difference between a dominant and a recessive allele. *(2 marks)*

b In pea plants, purple flowers are dominant (P) and white flowers are recessive (p). A plant with the alleles Pp was crossed with another plant with the alleles pp.

Complete the following Punnett square to calculate the likelihood of one of the offspring having white flowers. *(3 marks)*

	Plant 1	
	P	p
Plant 2 P		
p		

14 a Describe how an organism can be genetically modified. *(3 marks)*

b Describe **two** advantages of producing products through genetic modification. *(4 marks)*

1 _____

2 _____

15 The graph shows the number of people who died due to different diseases caused by smoking.

number of deaths × 100 000 vs *disease type*
- heart disease: 9
- lung disease: 12
- lung and throat cancer: 10
- stroke: 5
- other respiratory problems: 3

a Name the addictive drug in tobacco smoke. *(1 mark)*

b How many people died due to lung disease? *(1 mark)*

c Which disease type caused twice as many deaths as strokes? *(1 mark)*

d Explain why smoking increases the risk of suffering from a respiratory infection. *(4 marks)*

Section 3 Checklist

Revision question number	Outcome	Topic reference	☹	😐	🙂
1a	Name some recreational and medicinal drugs.	8.3.3			
1b	Name an effect of tobacco smoke on health.	8.3.5			
1c	Name an effect of alcohol on health or behaviour.	8.3.4			
1d	State whether alcohol affects conception or pregnancy. State whether or not tobacco smoke affects the development of a foetus.	8.3.4 8.3.5			
2	State what is meant by a gene.	10.4.1			
3	Describe the process of inhaling.	8.3.2			
4a	Name the parts of the digestive system.	8.4.4			
4b	State what is meant by digestion.	8.4.4			
5a	Name some nutrients in a diet.	8.4.1			
5b, c	State potential problems for someone with an unhealthy diet.	8.4.3			
6a	State the products of photosynthesis.	9.4.1			
6b	State where photosynthesis occurs in a plant.	9.4.1			
6c, d	Carry out an experiment to test for the presence of starch.	9.4.3			
7a	Name the parts of the gas exchange system.	8.3.1			
7b	Describe the role of the alveoli in gas exchange.	8.3.1			
7c	Describe how the parts of the gas exchange system are adapted to their function.	8.3.1			
8a	Calculate lung volume from the results of an experiment.	8.3.2			
8b	Describe the differences between inhaled and exhaled air.	8.3.1			
8c	Suggest factors that could affect lung volume.	8.3.2			
9a, b	Explain the role of each nutrient in the body.	8.4.1			
9c	Calculate energy requirements.	8.4.3			
9d	Describe how to test foods for the presence of sugars.	8.4.2			
10a, b	Describe the role of enzymes in digestion.	8.4.5			
10c	Describe the role of bacteria in digestion.	8.4.5			
11a	State the word equation for aerobic respiration.	9.3.1			
11b, c	Describe the differences between aerobic and anaerobic respiration.	9.3.2			
12	Describe the process of natural selection.	10.3.1			
13a	Describe the difference between dominant and recessive alleles.	10.4.3			
13b	Use a Punnett square to show what happens during a genetic cross.	10.4.3			
14a	Describe how an organism can be genetically modified.	10.4.4			
14b	Describe some advantages of producing products through genetic modification.	10.4.4			
15	Describe the effects of tobacco smoke on health.	8.3.5			

Answers

EP6
A 3
B toy car used, length of slope
C observational – 2, 3; pattern-seeking – 1, 4
D similar, repeatable, confidence

What you need to remember
data, measurements, independent, dependent, control, repeatable

EP7
A secondary data
B a 3   b 2   c 4   d 1
C repeat, same, the internet, conclusion

What you need to remember
best fit, same, secondary, conclusion

EP8
A 1 and 3
B We measured the height of the step using a 50 cm ruler.
C a3, b1, c2
D **four** from: use shorter sentences; correct spelling and grammar; include a diagram / equation; put information in a logical order; only include relevant information; use language suitable for intended audience

What you need to remember
effective, read, audience, purpose

EP9
A article, because the work has been peer reviewed but the video has probably not been reviewed by any experts; video: the person has probably been paid to say what the manufacturer wants
B Albie – likely to be under pressure from his boss to report that medicine is helpful and causes few side-effects / could report problems with the drug so that the project is extended Madison – more likely to report that a medicine is harmful, so that the website is successful
C peer review involves scientists who are experts in the same field checking whether the work is correct, making it less likely it is inaccurate or includes a mistake

What you need to remember
evidence, peer review, journal, funder, bias

EP10
A claim – a statement that says that something is true; evidence – this consists of the measurements, data, or observations that support or oppose a claim; reasoning – ideas about what evidence means, in the form of an argument for or against a claim
B a A substance in coffee, acrylamide, makes you more likely to get cancer.
   b Lab rats that drank a mixture of water and acrylamide grew cancer tumours.
   c there was no pattern in the results; for example, there were no more people with cancer in the group that drank the most coffee than in the group that drank the least coffee
C opinion: e.g. coffee does not need a cancer warning; justification: e.g. there were no more people with cancer in the group that drank the most coffee than in the group who drank the least coffee and even though lab rats that consumed acrylamide grew cancer tumours, rats and humans digest acrylamide differently

What you need to remember
true, evidence, observations, argument, evidence

EP11
A might benefit – 2, 3, 4; will not benefit – 1, 5
B a lose jobs / income
   b e.g. fewer greenhouse gases / less pollution from delivery vans
   c e.g. good idea – hospital worker might get medicines delivered more quickly / people might get orders delivered more quickly; bad idea – delivery van drivers might lose jobs / income, people under flight-paths might suffer from noise pollution / risks of drones falling from the sky
C e.g. benefits – less likely to get ill, will not have to take time off school / work; risks and disadvantages – the vaccine may have unwanted side-effects, may be prohibitively expensive for some people

What you need to remember
benefits, different, risks

EP12
A model – a way of representing something that is too difficult to display, usually because it is too big, too small, or too complicated; theory – an explanation for patterns in observations or data that is supported by evidence; law – a statement that describes a pattern or rule about something that happens that is always true. It does not explain *why* something happens
B Big Bang, kinetic, combustion, evolution, germ
C 2, 4, 5, 6, 8

What you need to remember
explanation, evidence, kinetic, Big Bang, evidence

EP13
A reason to change a theory – a, b, d, f; longer to accept a new theory – c, e
B does not, correct, argumentation
C scientists might test a new theory – by trying to find out why it may be wrong; a new theory might be wrong – if there are observations or data that do not support it; if scientists have looked for, but not found, evidence that contradicts a new theory, – then the new theory is stronger than it would otherwise be

What you need to remember

theory, new, evidence, conferences / meetings, correct, tested, correct, argumentation

Enquiry Processes Pinchpoint

A   this is an incorrect answer – although the investigation **may** work, you will not know which variables made the difference
B   this is an incorrect answer – you need to **change** the independent variable, **measure** the dependent variable and **control** all the other variables
C   this is the correct answer
D   this is an incorrect answer – repeatability increases the confidence in a conclusion; all investigations **should** be repeated

Pinchpoint follow-up

A   independent – what you change in an investigation; dependent – what you measure or observe in an investigation; control – what you keep the same in an investigation
B   independent, control, control, dependent, control
C   variables include: amount of light / shade, temperature, weather, pH, type of soil, substances washed in by rain
D   1, 4, 6, 7

1.3.1

A   water resistance – must push many liquid particles out of the way – a dolphin swimming; air resistance – must push many gas particles out of the way – a bird flying; friction – rough surfaces are touching – brakes on a bus
B   water resistance causes boat to slow; to reduce friction between metal parts; without friction your shoe would slip uselessly on the pavement, like on ice; air resistance causes the skydiver to fall more slowly
C   a   weight (gravity)
    b   air resistance (drag due to air)
    c   continue moving with same speed in the same direction

What you need to remember

friction, rough, lubrication, air, water (either order), streamlined, slow down, contact, resultant, equilibrium, stationary, same, direction, newton

1.3.2

A   deforms, compress, stretch
B   2, 1, 4, 3
C   10 cm
D   a

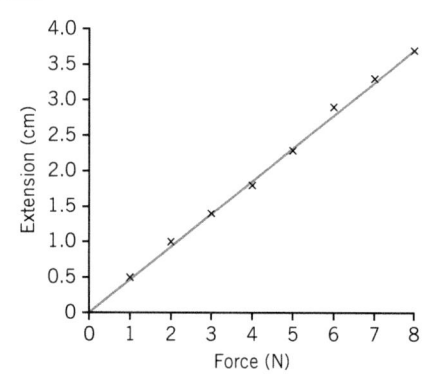

b   yes
c   the graph is a straight line through origin / force has a linear relationship to extension (or other way round) / force is proportional to extension.

What you need to remember

deform, compress, pushes, reaction, stretch, extension, tension, double, Hooke's Law, proportional, elastic, linear, linear, origin

1.3.3

A   when an object is in equilibrium the sum of the clockwise moments is equal to the sum of the anticlockwise moments
B   a $5.0 \times 0.50 = 2.5$ N m   b $50 \times 0.40 = 20$ N m
    c   centre of gravity is where their weight acts; if the line of action of the person's weight falls outside the narrow rope, they will topple as the weight will act as a turning force and pull them over

What you need to remember

pivot, moment, moment, force, distance, pivot, newton metre, force, pivot, moment, equilibrium, law of moments, weight, above, below (either order), no, topple

1.4.1

A   a   same number of particles packed into smaller space, with longer arrows
    b   must withstand lots of collisions with air particles
B   a   an increase in temperature – causes an increase in pressure – because the gas particles move faster, so collide harder and more often; an increase in volume – causes a decrease in pressure – because the particles have further to travel so collide less often
    b   pressure $= \dfrac{24}{1.5} = 16 \text{N/m}^2$
C   pressure decreases with height; less oxygen so harder to breathe / can cause altitude sickness

What you need to remember

fluid, gas pressure, particles, compressed, density, force, area, newtons per square metre, force, pressure, atmospheric pressure, atmospheric pressure, smaller / less

1.4.2

A   a   boat – float, pebble – sink, basketball – float
    b   float: density of object < density of water; sink: density of object > density of water
B   a   larger pressure the deeper you go; at surface, same as atmospheric pressure
    b   pressure $= \dfrac{\text{force}}{\text{area}} = \dfrac{750\,000}{2.4} = 310\,000 \text{N/m}^2$ (to 2 sig. fig.)
C   a   upwards arrow from where ship touches water labelled upthrust (or buoyancy); downwards arrow from same place, same length, labelled weight (or gravity)

b upwards short arrow from middle of anchor labelled upthrust (or buoyancy); downwards long arrow from same place labelled weight (or gravity)

What you need to remember
liquid pressure, pressure, upthrust, density, incompressible

1.4.3
A a lying flat: $\dfrac{20}{0.12} = 170\,\text{N/m}^2$ (to 2 sig. fig.)

on its end: $\dfrac{20}{0.060} = 330\,\text{N/m}^2$ (to 2 sig. fig.)

b $\dfrac{3 \times 20}{0.12} = 500\,\text{N/m}^2$

B a $\dfrac{5.0}{0.010} = 500\,\text{N/m}^2$

b $\dfrac{2500}{6.4} = 390\,\text{N/m}^2$ (to 2 sig. fig.)

C with narrow heel, person's weight is concentrated on small area so stress is greater and marks made in wood; with wider heel, larger area for same weight so stress is less and no marks in wood

What you need to remember
stress, force, surface area, newtons per square metre, force, stress, large, small, stress, larger, less

Big Idea 1 Pinchpoint
A this is an incorrect answer – a change in temperature is not needed for there to be a change in pressure
B this is the correct answer
C this is an incorrect answer – if everything else is the same, then a smaller surface area means a **larger** pressure
D this is an incorrect answer – the amount of gas is fixed because the air is trapped, so there are the same number of gas particles

Pinchpoint follow-up
A a twice as many collisions between particles, and between particles and container walls, in bottle **Y**
b pressure is twice as high in bottle **Y**
B a compressing the gas makes it denser, gas particles collide more often, so pressure is higher; the pressure is then higher than the air inside the tyre, so pushes into it
b pulling the plunger back spreads the gas particles out inside the syringe – makes it less dense, the gas particles collide less often as there are fewer of them in each cm³, so pressure is lower; the atmospheric pressure is now higher outside syringe, so air from outside pushes in
C a pressure $= \dfrac{\text{force}}{\text{area}}$

b pressure $= \dfrac{\text{force}}{\text{area}} = \dfrac{10}{2.4} = 4.2\,\text{N/m}^2$

c pressure $= \dfrac{\text{force}}{\text{area}} = \dfrac{10}{1.2} = 8.3\,\text{N/m}^2$

d as area increases, pressure decreases: if you double area you halve pressure
D a increases
b proportional – doubling (increasing) density doubles (increases) pressure
c inversely proportional – doubling (increasing) volume halves (decreases) pressure
d pressure increases because the same amount of gas is squeezed into a smaller volume, increasing its density

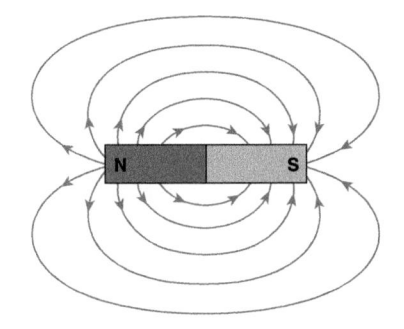

2.3.1
A a

b similar diagram to part **a**, but twice as many field lines
B a attract **b** attract **c** repel **d** repel
C curved field lines like **A a**, pointing from magnetic south to magnetic north

What you need to remember
magnets, magnetic materials, iron, iron, north pole, south pole (either order), north, Earth's, south, different / opposite, same, magnetic field, magnetic field lines, more, force

2.4.1
A a electromagnets can be turned off; permanent magnets cannot
b wire in a coil surrounding a core, connected in series with a power supply (or labelled with current flowing through the coil) and a switch
B **two** from: increase number of turns on the coil; increase current flowing in the wire / increase the power supply potential difference; use a magnetic material in the core
C a electric field – charge; magnetic field – current in a wire; gravitational field – mass
b decreases
D e.g. build an electromagnet with an iron core to pick up steel paper clips; vary how much current flows through coil; count how many paper clips it picks up for each current

What you need to remember
coil, turns / loops, core, more turns, current, material, magnetise, permanent, turned off, field, bar, solenoid

2.4.2
A clockwise from left: electromagnet, iron armature, make and break switch, spring metal strip
B 2, 1, 3, 4

C levitate train; propel train; in scrapyards to lift a car (or other heavy metal object); sort metal for recycling; electric motor

D if a large current passes through the electromagnet; the magnetic field of the electromagnet is strong enough to attract the iron catch; the catch moves down and breaks the circuit

What you need to remember
current, coil, iron, bell, iron, current, coil, current, coil, magnet

Big Idea 2 Pinchpoint
A this is the correct answer

B this is an incorrect answer – it is the **current** from the phone that makes the coil act as an electromagnet, which then makes the diaphragm move

C this is an incorrect answer – it is the current from the **phone** that makes the coil act as an electromagnet

D this is an incorrect answer – it is a **magnetic** force that acts from the permanent magnet on the coil

Pinchpoint follow-up
A visitor presses switch and completes a circuit, so current flows; current flows in the electromagnet, attracting the iron armature; that breaks the circuit so current stops flowing; the iron armature springs back to its original position, ringing the bell once; the circuit is complete again, so the process starts again, until the visitor lets go of the switch

B potential difference, current, electromagnet, coil, cone, cone, cone, sound

C 4, 5, 6, 2, 1, 3

D gravitational – Moon orbits Earth – mass; electrical – lighting a bulb – charge; magnetic – fridge magnet – electromagnet or permanent magnet

3.3.1
A lever, smaller, greater, multiplier, smaller, conserves

B 750 × 20 = 15 000 J or 15 kJ

C **a** 120 × 0.40 = 48 J
  b 48 J (same as for **a**), because machines conserve energy

What you need to remember
work, displacement, energy, done, joule, force, work, energy, more / greater, simple machines, levers, gears (either order)

3.4.1
A °C, stays the same, increases, move / vibrate, J, thermal, increases

B **a** the water particles vibrate more, but do not move past each other
  b the water particles vibrate more and move past each other faster

C **a** soup – temperature decreases; air – temperature increases
  b hot object heats colder object until both reach same temperature

What you need to remember
temperature, thermometer, degrees Celsius, °C, same, equilibrium, no, more, thermal, mass, type (either order)

3.4.2
A reduce, slower, insulators

B **a** particles heated, vibrate more; collide with neighbours and make them vibrate more; energy transferred from hotter place to colder place
  b particles heated, vibrate and move apart; liquid becomes hotter and less dense and rises; energy transferred from hotter place to colder place; colder more dense liquid sinks to take its place and be heated

C best conductor will transfer energy the fastest, so wax will melt fastest, recording shortest time; copper is the best conductor; glass is an insulator; aluminium is a conductor

What you need to remember
thermal, hot, cooler / colder / cold, vibrate, conduction, solid, gaseous / gas, insulators, dense, dense, sinks, convection, convection current

3.4.3
A **a** black absorbs infrared better than white, so black clothes warm up and dry faster
  b matt surfaces absorb infrared better than shiny ones and black surfaces absorb more infrared than any other colour, so matt black surfaces heat the water faster

B **a** conduction – in solids, particles vibrating and colliding with neighbours; convection – particles moving from a hotter place to a colder place; radiation – emission and absorption of infrared radiation
  b hot objects emit infrared radiation; when an object absorbs this radiation, it causes heating

C **a** **i** plastic is a good thermal insulator
    ii foam contains pockets of air which can't move
    iii shiny surface reflects infrared radiation
  b **i** conduction
    ii convection
    iii radiation

What you need to remember
conduction, convection, radiation, infrared radiation, thermal imaging camera, absorb, transmitted / absorbed / reflected (any order) × 3, black / dark, matt / dull, white / light, shiny / gloss

Big Idea 3 Pinchpoint
A this is an incorrect answer – energy is transferred from **hotter** objects to colder ones

B this is the correct answer

C this is an incorrect answer – solids do not pass on energy by convection, they **conduct**

D this is an incorrect answer – the process described is correct, but it is called **conduction**

Pinchpoint follow-up

A vibrate, liquids, gases, forces, vibrating, pushes, vibrate, kinetic, rise, conduction

B   **a** poor insulators: electrons free to move, transfer energy quickly
  b good insulators: no free electrons to transfer energy
  c good insulators: mostly gas, which is a poor conductor

C solid – particles fixed in position, can only vibrate, so cannot pass on energy by convection; liquid – packed close together but able to slide past each other so can pass on energy by convection; gas – spaced far apart and free to move so can pass on energy by convection

D conduction – when solid is heated, particles vibrate more, transmitting vibrations to their neighbours; convection – when liquid or gas is heated, particles move apart so that it becomes less dense and rises with the particles moving to a new position, transferring energy as they move; can only happen in liquids and gases; radiation – emission and absorption of infrared, can happen through a vacuum

4.3.1

A   **a** clockwise from top-left: sound waves, magnet, coil, diaphragm
  b clockwise from left: diaphragm (or cone), magnet, coil, sound waves
  c microphone – absorbs – output – pressure into potential difference; loudspeaker – input – emits – potential difference into pressure

B   **a** more   **b** more

C the sound wave causes the whole diaphragm to vibrate in and out; this vibration causes the coil to move near the magnet; which varies the potential difference

What you need to remember

compressions, rarefactions, pressure, microphone, loudspeaker, 20 000, ultrasound

4.3.2

A radio waves, microwaves, infrared, visible light, ultraviolet, X-rays, gamma rays

B   **a** e.g. radio waves – TV signals; microwaves – mobile phones, microwave ovens; infrared - heating, cooking; ultraviolet – detecting forgeries; X-rays - seeing broken bones; gamma rays – killing cancer cells
  b continuous (spectrum); all same type of wave, but have different frequencies / wavelengths / energy

C infrared has low frequency and transfers little energy when absorbed; it causes heating in the body; ultraviolet has high frequency and transfers a lot of energy when absorbed; it causes ionisation in the body, which can cause a mutation in DNA, sometimes leading to cancer

What you need to remember

electromagnetic spectrum, visible light, Sun, wavelengths, high, high, wavelength, low, low, long, gamma, ionise, cancer, microwaves

4.4.1

A   **a** (clockwise from top-left) amplitude, peak or crest, wavelength, trough
  b transverse

B   **a** fix one end of spring, bounce wave off it
  b one bit of the spring oscillating causes the next bit to start oscillating
  c pulse gets a bit smaller as it goes along because of friction

C   **a** across the surface of the water
  b up and down, at right angles to the direction of the wave

D Two waves that are out of step superpose so they cancel out to produce a smaller wave. An incident wave hits a barrier so it reflects to produce a reflected wave. Two waves that are in step superpose so they add up to produce a larger wave.

What you need to remember

wave, energy, transverse, longitudinal, transmission, superpose

Big Idea 4 Pinchpoint

A this is an incorrect answer – **no** part of the spring moves along the whole length of the spring

B this is the correct answer

C this is an incorrect answer – energy **is** transferred by the wave

D this is an incorrect answer – the wave is **transverse**

Pinchpoint follow-up

A   **a** from left: oscillations, wavelength, energy transfer
  b the particles oscillate across at right angles to the length of the spring, while energy is transferred along the spring

B transverse – wave moves at right angles to the oscillation; electromagnetic wave (light) / water wave / earthquake waves that cannot travel in liquid rock; longitudinal – wave moves parallel to the oscillation; sound / ultrasound / earthquake waves that can travel in solid or liquid rock

C along, waves, damage, work

D   **a** particles oscillate parallel to direction of wave
  b particles oscillate at right angles to the direction of the wave

Section 1 Revision questions

1   **a** two waves in step will add up and produce a bigger wave (larger amplitude) [1]; two waves out of step will produce a smaller wave (smaller amplitude) [1]
  b **i** 60 cm [1]   **ii** 0 cm [1]

2   **a** extension is **proportional** to force (or vice versa) (or when force **doubled**, extension **doubles**) [1]
  b 4 cm [1]

3   a   separating metal for recycling [1]; motor for electrically powered train [1]
    b   separating metal – iron or steel attracted to electromagnet, other materials are not [1]; motor – magnetic field of electromagnet pushes against magnetic field of permanent magnet, gives force to move train [1] (**do not accept** electromagnet pushes against magnet)
4   a   transmitted through the air [1]; absorbed by the toast [1]; emitted from the heating element [1]
    b   degree Celsius (°C) [1]; joule (J) / kilojoule (kJ) / kilowatt hour (kW h) [1]
5   a   keeps moving with same speed [1] in the same direction [1]
    b   1 [1]
6   a   3 [1]
    b   which liquid [1], which gauge [1]
7   a 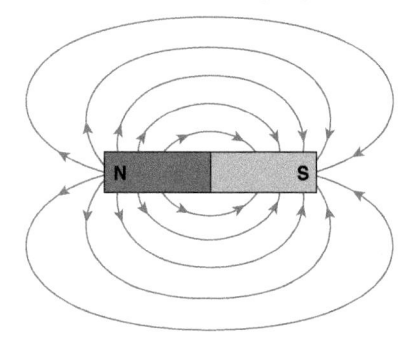
        correct direction [1], correct shape [1]
    b   3 [1]
8   cup pushes particles of table closer together [1]; bonds between particles are compressed [1]; bonds between particles push back and support cup [1]
9   a   transverse – oscillation (or motion of source or displacement) is at 90° (or right angles or perpendicular or normal) to the direction of the wave [1]; longitudinal – oscillation is parallel to direction of wave (or equivalent terms as above) [1]
    b   axes drawn & labelled [1], data plotted [1], best-fit curved line drawn [1]
10 **three** from: sound wave hits diaphragm (flexible plate) [1]; diaphragm vibrates [1]; moves a coil near a magnet [1]; produces an electrical signal [1]
11 $200 \times 3000 = 600\,000$ [1] J [1]
12 a   i   hot: Y, cold: X [1]   ii Y [1]
    b   i   hot air inside the balloon is less dense than the air around / outside the balloon [1], so the air inside the balloon has a smaller mass and weight than the air around / outside the balloon [1]
        ii long upwards arrow from middle of balloon, short downwards arrow from same place [1]
13 a   temperature [1], volume [1]
    b   pressure $= \dfrac{\text{force}}{\text{area}}$ [1]
    c   i $1.8 \times 0.5 = 0.90$ m² [1]
        ii $\dfrac{800}{0.90}$ [1] $= 890$ N/m² [1] (to 2 sig. fig.)
        iii no, he will not sink as $890 < 20\,000$ N/m² [1]
14 $\dfrac{30}{1000} = 0.030$ m [1]; $8.0 \times 0.030 = 0.24$ N m [1]
15 radiation [1], shiny surfaces emit less infrared [1]
16 a   C [1]
    b   **six** from: diagram shows coil [1], diaphragm (cone) attached to coil [1], (permanent) magnet [1]; phone causes current in coil [1]; coil acts as electromagnet [1]; magnet causes magnetic force, pushing coil [1]; moves diaphragm (cone) in and out [1], emitting sound as it pushes air [1]

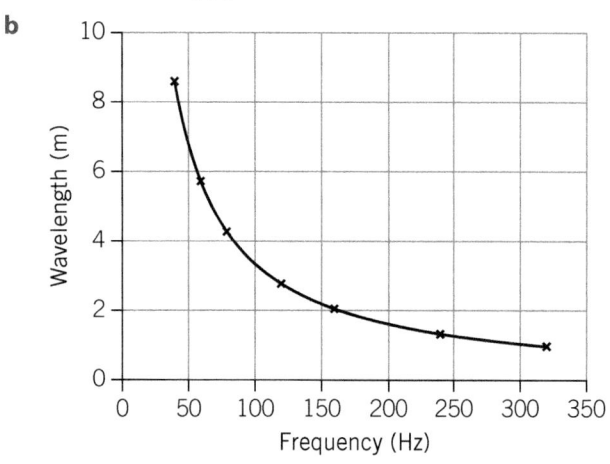

5.3.1

A   1   Every material, and everything in the Universe, is made up of **one** or more elements.
    2   It is **impossible** to break down an element into other substances.
    3   The chemical symbol of magnesium is **Mg**.
    4   The chemical symbol of sodium is **Na**.
    5   Scientists in the UK and Russia use **the same symbol** for the element iron.
B   aluminium – Al; bromine – Br; carbon – C; chlorine – Cl; copper – Cu; gold – Au; hydrogen – H; iodine – I; iron – Fe
C   potassium; Mg; N; sodium; O; S; tungsten; Zn

What you need to remember

substances, elements, Periodic, chemical, symbol

5.3.2

A   An atom is the smallest part of an element that can exist. The atoms of copper are all the same as each other. A single atom of the element copper does not have the properties of a piece of copper.
B   elements – W and Y; not elements – X and Z
C   smallest, mercury, mercury, many

What you need to remember

atoms, smallest, atoms, different, many

5.3.3

A   from top: compound, element, atom, molecule
B   an element, an element, two, a compound, different from, yellow, grey, magnetic, not magnetic, joined

C a elements – top left and bottom right
b compounds – top right and bottom left

What you need to remember
two, strongly, different, one, molecule

5.3.4

A magnesium oxide – MgO – magnesium and oxygen
sodium chloride – NaCl – sodium and chlorine
carbon dioxide – CO$_2$ – carbon and oxygen
sulfur dichloride – SCl$_2$ – sulfur and chlorine
calcium sulfate – CaSO$_4$ – calcium, sulfur, and oxygen

B (left, from top) H$_2$, H$_2$O; (right from top) CO$_2$ and CH$_4$

C ethanoic acid – 2, 4, 2, 0; ethanol – 2, 6, 1, 0; paracetamol – 8, 9, 1, 2; ibuprofen – 13, 18, 2, 0

What you need to remember
chemical, number, oxygen, one

5.3.5

A **long** molecules; **identical** groups; **many** different polymers; **smaller** molecules

B poly(propene) is used to make ropes because it is strong and flexible; nylon can be used to make artificial heart valves because it is strong and flexible, does not wear away, and is not damaged by blood; cotton is used to make clothes because it can be spun into flexible threads that can be woven into cloth; Kevlar® is used to make bullet-proof vests that police officers can wear all day because it is strong and lightweight

C PETE and rigid PVC because both are waterproof and rigid

What you need to remember
long, many, many, different, atoms

5.4.1

A bars should be correctly and neatly plotted
B top, bottom, decreases, below, 29
C from top to bottom of Group 3, density increases; from top to bottom of Group 4, density increases; the pattern in density is similar for Group 3 and Group 4; from bottom to top of Group 4, density decreases

What you need to remember
groups, periods, groups, periods, group

5.4.2

A left – bubbles of gas; right, from top – purple flame, potassium, water and universal indicator
B **similar** reactions; **hydrogen** gas is made; get **more** vigorous; is **more** vigorous; a **chemical** property; a **physical** property; **there is** a pattern
C increases, less than, 0.26

What you need to remember
left, alkali, conduct, shiny, vigorously, new, hydrogen, hydroxide

5.4.3

A top symbol – toxic – difficulty breathing – use in a fume cupboard
bottom symbol – corrosive – burns eyes – wear safety goggles

B darker, top, iodine, solid, dark

C 1 true; 2 true; 3 false; 4 true

What you need to remember
right, halogens, metals, pattern / trend, reactions, chloride, displaces

5.4.4

A U, V, Z
B 2, 4, 6
C a Xe, Kr, Ar, Ne, He
b balloons filled with argon, xenon, and krypton sink

What you need to remember
right, noble, metals, unreactive (inert)

Big Idea 5 Pinchpoint

A this is an incorrect answer – sodium is **not** the most reactive element in Group 1 and chlorine is **not** the most reactive element in Group 7

B this is the correct answer

C this is an incorrect answer – potassium is **less** reactive than the elements below it in its group and chlorine **less** reactive than fluorine in its group

D this is an incorrect answer – the patterns in reactivity are **different** for different groups of the Periodic Table: in Groups 1 and 2, the elements get more reactive from top to bottom; in Group 7, the elements get less reactive from top to bottom

Pinchpoint follow-up

A a different, bottom, Group 1, most, top, Group 1, least, top, Group 7, most, bottom, Group 7, less
b iron, bromine, iron, iodide; chlorine, chlorine
c hydrogen, water, potassium hydroxide; lithium, lithium

B a 2, 3, 4, 1
b i calcium, calcium bromide, strontium bromide
ii reaction between strontium and bromine

C a 2, 4, 5
b 1 – most vigorous reaction is between caesium and **fluorine**; 3 – the reaction of lithium and fluorine is **less** vigorous; 6 – the reaction of rubidium and iodine is **less** vigorous

D lithium is at the top of Group 1 so it is the least reactive element in its group; fluorine is at the top of Group 7 so it is the most reactive element in its group; caesium is at the bottom of Group 1 so it is the most reactive element in its group; iodine is near the bottom of Group 7 so it is the least reactive element in its group

6.3.1

A
- **a** sulfur + oxygen ⟶ sulfur dioxide
- **b** sodium + chlorine ⟶ sodium chloride
- **c** methane + oxygen ⟶ carbon dioxide + water

B
- **a** oxygen and hydrogen (in either order)
- **b** water
- **c** 4   **d** 4   **e** 2   **f** 2

C 2, 4

What you need to remember
reactants, products, left, right, atoms, differently, after

6.3.2

A fuel – a material that burns to transfer energy by heating; combustion – a reaction with oxygen in which energy is transferred to the surroundings as heat and light; renewable fuel – a fuel that can be produced over a short timescale; non-renewable fuel – a fuel that cannot be replaced once it has been used

B (from top) carbon dioxide; water; carbon dioxide and water

C
- **a** independent variable – fuel; dependent variable – increase in temperature of water; control variables – volume of water, distance of flame from test tube
- **b i** fuel   **ii** increase in temperature of water

What you need to remember
energy, combustion, oxygen, carbon dioxide, water

6.3.3

A 1, 2, 4, 5

B copper carbonate decomposed most quickly; lead carbonate decomposed more slowly than copper carbonate; potassium carbonate did not decompose

C
- **a** W and Z
- **b** in each chosen reaction, there is one reactant and two products

What you need to remember
one, two, compound, compounds, oxide, carbon dioxide, thermal

6.3.4

A equal to, melting, does not change, conservation

B the same numbers of each type of atom are present before and after the reaction.

C magnesium, magnesium oxide, increased, gas, the same as, 0.08 g

What you need to remember
joined, change, equal, conservation, physical

6.4.1

A (top row) 8; (bottom row) 25

B increase, exothermic, more, more

C 1 – physical change, endothermic; 2 – chemical reaction, exothermic; 3 – chemical reaction, endothermic

What you need to remember
energy, exothermic, transferred, endothermic, surroundings, energy, to, from

6.4.2

A 2, 3

B R

C ethanol – X; hydrogen – Z; petrol – Y

What you need to remember
products, after, exothermic, endothermic

6.4.3

A top row – process requires energy from surroundings, endothermic; bottom – process transfers energy to surroundings, exothermic

B from top – Y, Z, X

C more, from, endothermic

What you need to remember
break, endothermic, products, exothermic, more, less, catalyst

Big Idea 6 Pinchpoint

A this is an incorrect answer – the total mass of reactants is **not** different from the total mass of product

B this is the correct answer

C this is an incorrect answer – the reactants and products do **not** have the same properties

D this is an incorrect answer – the total mass of products is **not** less than the total mass of reactants

Pinchpoint follow-up

A gas, eight, four, two, eight, the same number of, the same number of, equal to

B
- **a i** 12.8   **ii** 4.4   **iii** 10.0
- **b** there are the same number of atoms of each element in the reactants and products; this means that the total mass of products is equal to the total mass of reactants, for every chemical reaction

C
- **a** 2, 4, 6
- **b** 1 – there are **two** nitrogen atoms in the reactants; 3 – the atoms are joined together **differently**; 5 – the properties of a substance **depend on** how its atoms are joined together

D one of the reactants, sulfur, is in the solid state; one of the reactants, oxygen, is in the gas state; the product, sulfur dioxide, is in the gas state; when the chemical reaction occurs, atoms are rearranged; when the chemical reaction occurs, atoms are not destroyed; when the chemical reaction occurs, atoms join together differently; the mass of an atom never changes, even when it is in a substance that is in the gas state; the total mass of atoms in the reactants is equal to the total mass of atoms in the product

Big Idea 7 Answers

7.3.1
A argon – 1; carbon dioxide – 0.04; nitrogen – 78; oxygen – 21
B the greenhouse effect, global warming, methane, carbon dioxide
C from left: 3, 2, 4, 1
D 2

What you need to remember
atmosphere, transferred, dioxide, temperature

7.3.2
A oceans, fossil fuels, the atmosphere, some sedimentary rocks
B atmosphere, did not change, increased, faster
C **removes** CO_2 from the atmosphere – photosynthesis by plants, the formation of some sedimentary rocks, dissolving in the oceans, the formation of coal and other fossil fuels; **adds** CO_2 to the atmosphere – respiration by plants, respiration by animals, burning petrol in cars, burning diesel in cars

What you need to remember
sinks, sedimentary, fossil, cycle, respire, burn / combust, photosynthesis, dissolving, same, change / increase / decrease

7.3.3
A global warming; climate change; deforestation; greenhouse effect
B deforestation – less carbon dioxide is removed from the atmosphere; burning fossil fuels – more carbon dioxide goes into the atmosphere; every year, more carbon dioxide is added to the atmosphere than is removed – the concentration of carbon dioxide in the atmosphere increases; climate change – glaciers melt, some plant and animal species become extinct, it is harder for humans in some areas to grow enough food
C 1, 2, 3, 5

What you need to remember
cycle, carbon, temperature, warming, warming, ice, weather, climate, species, food

7.4.1
A cannot, the same, more, strongly
B **a** carbon
 b copper, iron, lead, zinc
 c the metals chosen are below carbon in the reactivity series
C **a** aluminium is above carbon in the reactivity series, so cannot be extracted by heating with carbon
 b 1↑, 2↓, 3↓, 4↓, 5↓, 6↑

What you need to remember
crust, mixed, ore, below, electrolysis

7.4.2
A 2, 3
B 1, 5, 4, 2, 3
C advantages – 1, 3, 4; disadvantages – 2, 5
D **a** low-density poly(ethene) and poly(propene) will float in water, while the other two will not
 b the independent variable is categoric

What you need to remember
processing, reducing

Big Idea 7 Pinchpoint
A this is an incorrect answer – it is **global warming** that occurs only if processes 2 and 3 occur faster than processes 1 and 4
B this is an incorrect answer – both the rate at which carbon dioxide is added to the atmosphere **and** the rate at which it is removed determine whether or not global warming occurs
C this is the correct answer
D this is an incorrect answer – to decide whether or not global warming will occur, it is necessary to compare the rates at which carbon dioxide is added to the atmosphere (arrows 2 and 3) to the rates at which it is being removed (arrows 1 and 4)

Pinchpoint follow-up
A climate change – changes to long-term weather patterns; global warming – the gradual increase in the average surface temperature of the Earth; greenhouse effect – when energy from the Sun is transferred to the thermal energy store of gases in the Earth's atmosphere, keeping the surface of the Earth warmer than it would otherwise be; greenhouse gas – a substance that contributes to the greenhouse effect, such as carbon dioxide
B 3, 4, 7, 8
C **a** 1 – photosynthesis; 2 – respiration; 3 – combustion; 4 – dissolving
 b humans have burned increasing amounts of fossils fuels; combustion releases carbon dioxide into the atmosphere, which is a greenhouse gas; greenhouse gases contribute to the greenhouse effect, and thus to global warming
D sinks, sedimentary, cycle, respiration, combustion, photosynthesis, faster

Section 2 Revision questions
1 nitrogen [1]
2 reactants [1]
3 New substances are made. [1] Atoms are rearranged and join together differently. [1]
4 hydrogen [1] and sodium hydroxide [1]
5 **a** bars correctly drawn [1]
 b from top to bottom of the group, melting point increases [1]
6 poly(propene) [1]

7　a　Al [1]
　　b　a substance that is made of one type of atom [1] that cannot be broken down into new substances [1]
　　c　the appearance of a compound is different from the appearance of the elements it is made from [1]
8　(from top) N_2 [1], NO [1], NO_2 [1], O_3 [1]
9　a　the diagram shows nitrogen reacting with oxygen to make an oxide [1]
　　b　decomposition [1]
　　c　2 in each box [1]
　　d　there are the same number of atoms of each element before and after the reaction [1]
10　a　2 [1]
　　b　(2 × 10) = 20 [1]
11　X is an element [1] but Y is a compound [1]; a molecule of X is made up of two atoms [1] but a molecule of Y is made up of three atoms [1]
12　a　X [1]　b　W [1]　c　Y [1] and Z [1]
　　d　W [1]　e　W [1]
13　a　the mixture glows bright red [1]
　　b　mass of reactants = mass of products
　　　　mass of bromine + mass of iron = mass of iron bromide
　　　　mass of bromine = mass of iron bromide − mass of iron
　　　　　　　　　　　　= 5.3 g − 1 g [1]
　　　　　　　　　　　　= 4.3 g [1]
14　burning fossil fuels adds carbon dioxide to the atmosphere [1]; carbon dioxide is a greenhouse gas [1]; increasing amounts of carbon dioxide in the atmosphere increase the thermal energy store of the atmosphere [1]; this results in global warming [1]; this results in ice caps / glaciers melting [1]; this results in sea levels rising [1]
15　a　electrolysis because lithium is more reactive / higher in the reactivity series than carbon [1]
　　b　magnesium and aluminium [1]
　　c　like lithium, magnesium and aluminium are also more reactive / higher in the reactivity series than carbon [1]
16　a　hydrogen and fluorine [1]
　　b　hydrogen fluoride [1]
　　c　exothermic [1], because the energy required to break bonds in the reactants is less than the energy released on making bonds in the products, so overall energy is transferred to the surroundings [1]

8.3.1

A　1 trachea; 2 lungs; 3 rib; 4 diaphragm; 5 bronchi; 6 bronchiole; 7 alveoli
B　Alveoli walls are only one cell thick. Alveoli create a large surface area.
C

Gas	Inhaled air	Exhaled air
carbon dioxide	less	more
nitrogen	same	same
oxygen	more	less

What you need to remember

respiratory, lungs, oxygen, exhale, trachea, bronchi / bronchus, alveoli / alveolus, gas exchange

8.3.2

A　rubber – diaphragm; balloon – lung; bell jar – chest cavity; tube – trachea
B　contract, up and out, contracts, down, increases, decreases, into
C　6, 2, 4, 5, 3, 1

What you need to remember

ribs, contract, increases, decreases, relax, decreases, increases, out, bell jar, asthma, volume

8.3.3

A　medicinal – antibiotic, paracetamol, aspirin, ibuprofen; recreational – ecstasy, caffeine, alcohol, tobacco
B　1 medicinal; 2 recreational; 3 recreational; 4 medicinal
C　alcohol – slows down the nervous system and damages the liver; tobacco – significantly increases risk of lung cancer and heart disease; caffeine – speeds up the nervous system
D　a　when someone becomes dependent on a drug and needs to keep taking it to feel normal
　　b　**two** from: headaches, sweating, anxiety

What you need to remember

drugs, recreational, medicinal, addiction, withdrawal symptoms

8.3.4

A　feeling relaxed and happy, difficulty walking and talking (drunk), unconsciousness, death
B　liver, brain
C　ethanol, bloodstream, nervous, depressant, slows down
D　1 true; 2 true; 3 false; 4 true

What you need to remember

ethanol, nervous, depressant, liver, unit, alcoholic(s)

8.3.5

A　lung cancer, heart attack, stroke
B　nicotine, tar, nicotine, tar, carbon monoxide
C　low birth weight baby, miscarriage during pregnancy
D　a　tobacco smoke damages the walls of the alveoli / excessive coughing up of mucus because of damage to the cilia damages the alveoli; less oxygen can pass into blood because there are fewer functional alveoli
　　b　arteries become blocked; poor blood flow to heart muscle can cause a heart attack

What you need to remember

cancer / disease, heart, passive, airways, monoxide, oxygen, stimulant, miscarriage

8.4.1

A lipid, protein, vitamin, carbohydrate
B protein – fish; vitamins and minerals – fruit; carbohydrate – pasta; lipid – butter
C carbohydrate – main source of energy; lipid – store of energy, keep you warm, protect organs; protein – growth and repair of body tissues; water – needed in all cells and body fluids; vitamin – needed in tiny amounts to keep you healthy
D 1 false; 2 true; 3 true; 4 false

What you need to remember

balanced, nutrients, carbohydrates, lipids (either order), proteins, vitamins, minerals (either order), fibre

8.4.2

A the solution changes colour
B pestle and mortar; pipette; filter paper; water bath
C filter paper, to the light, goes translucent
D starch – orange iodine solution – blue-black colour; sugar – blue Benedict's solution – brick-red colour; protein – blue copper sulfate and sodium hydroxide solution – purple colour; lipid – ethanol – cloudy, white layer

What you need to remember

food tests, iodine, starch, red, purple, protein, cloudy

8.4.3

A energy, joules, different, more
B 3, 2, 4, 1
C obesity – eating too much food or too many fatty foods; deficiency – lack of vitamin or mineral; starvation – eating too little food
D obese – diabetes, heart disease; underweight – lack of energy, poor immune system

What you need to remember

malnourishment, underweight, deficiency, starvation, fat, obese

8.4.4

A large, broken down, small
B clockwise from top: gullet, stomach, large intestine, rectum, small intestine
C small intestine, anus, stomach, gullet, large intestine

What you need to remember

digestive system, gullet, stomach, acid, digestion, small, large, rectum, anus

8.4.5

A protease, carbohydrase, lipase
B large intestine
C 1 false; 2 true; 3 true; 4 false
D carbohydrase – carbohydrate – sugars; protease – protein – amino acids; lipase – lipid – fatty acids and glycerol

What you need to remember

bacteria, vitamins, enzymes, catalyst, carbohydrase, sugar, protease, protein, lipase, glycerol, bile

Big Idea 8 Pinchpoint

A this is an incorrect answer – enzymes are **not** living and are **not** used up during a reaction
B this is an incorrect answer – carbohydrates are **not** broken down into amino acids, they are broken down into sugar molecules
C this is an incorrect answer – the **only** enzymes found in saliva are carbohydrases, which break down carbohydrates
D this is the correct answer

Pinchpoint follow-up

A Enzymes are catalysts. This means they are not used up in a reaction; Enzymes are catalysts. This means they speed up a reaction; Enzymes are made of protein molecules; Enzymes are not living as they cannot respire.
B carbohydrate – carbohydrase → individual squares drawn and labelled as sugar molecules; protein – protease → individual hexagons drawn and labelled as amino acids; lipid – lipase → rectangles drawn (some shaded) and labelled as fatty acids and glycerol molecule
C **a** carbohydrase – mouth, stomach, small intestine; protease – stomach, small intestine; lipase – small intestine
  b mouth, carbohydrate, carbohydrase, stomach, lipids, lipase, protein, protease
D many stains on clothes are food stains, enzymes will break down large food molecules (insoluble) into smaller molecules (soluble), easier to wash away; named example stated, e.g. grease stain is caused by lipids – lipase will break down lipid into fatty acids and glycerol

9.3.1

A respiration
B oxygen, carbon dioxide
C glucose, oxygen
D labelled arrow added pointing to a mitochondrion

What you need to remember

aerobic respiration, glucose, mitochondria, water, carbohydrates, plasma, haemoglobin

9.3.2

A glucose → lactic acid
B during intense / strenuous exercise, e.g. sprinting
C aerobic: glucose is a reactant; oxygen is a reactant; carbon dioxide is produced; water is produced; transfers more energy per glucose molecule
anaerobic: glucose is a reactant; lactic acid is produced
D 1 true; 2 false; 3 false; 4 true

What you need to remember

anaerobic respiration, lactic acid, oxygen debt, fermentation, ethanol

9.3.3

A yeast
B false, true, false, true
C glucose, ethanol
D 3, 4, 2, 5, 1

What you need to remember

yeast, beer / other alcoholic drink, fermentation, ethanol, enzymes, faster / quicker

9.4.1

A chloroplast
B glucose, oxygen
C water, light, oxygen
D carbon dioxide – enters through tiny holes on the underside of the leaf; water – diffuses into root hair cells; light – absorbed by chlorophyll in chloroplasts

What you need to remember

algae, producers, photosynthesis, consumers, water, glucose, chlorophyll

9.4.2

A (clockwise from top-left) waxy layer, chloroplast, palisade layer, spongy layer, air space, guard cell, stoma
B chloroplast – contains chlorophyll to trap sunlight; stomata – allow gases to diffuse into and out of leaf; guard cells – open and close stomata; veins – transport water to cells in leaf; waxy layer – reduces water loss through evaporation
C 1 false; 2 true; 3 false; 4 true

What you need to remember

leaves, stomata, carbon dioxide, oxygen, xylem, palisade, chloroplasts

9.4.3

A number of bubbles given off in a set time
B **two** from: light intensity, carbon dioxide concentration, water availability
C 4, 5, 3, 1, 2
D faster, slower, faster, stop, stops

What you need to remember

iodine, blue-black, oxygen / gas, light, carbon dioxide, temperature, increases

9.4.4

A nitrates, potassium
B NPK fertilisers
C nitrate – healthy growth – poor growth, older leaves are yellowed; phosphate – healthy roots – poor root growth, younger leaves look purple; potassium – healthy leaves and flowers – yellow leaves with dead patches; magnesium – making chlorophyll – plant leaves turn yellow
D soil, soil, root hair cells, xylem, amino acids, proteins

What you need to remember

minerals, magnesium, potassium, nitrates, phosphates, deficiency, fertilisers

Big Idea 9 Pinchpoint

A this is an incorrect answer – this is the word equation for **photosynthesis**
B this is an incorrect answer – aerobic respiration **also** occurs in plants and microorganisms
C this is the correct answer
D this is an incorrect answer – this is what happens when you breathe; respiration is **a chemical reaction**

Pinchpoint follow-up

A a glucose and oxygen underlined
  b carbon dioxide and water circled
  c glucose + oxygen (either order) → carbon dioxide + water (either order)
B a animal – aerobic respiration: plant – aerobic respiration, photosynthesis; microorganism – aerobic respiration, some species can photosynthesise
  b respire, movement, growth, plants, bacteria, photosynthesise, glucose
C a to contract to cause movement
  b to move tail so it can 'swim' to egg
  c to enable it to move by spinning flagella; move towards light to maximise photosynthesis
D glucose, digestion, small, diffuses, inhale, breathing, alveoli, carbon dioxide, exhaled

10.3.1

A changes in species over time
B pale, camouflaged, dark, pale, increasing, dark, pale, decreasing, increasing, dark
C 4, 6, 2, 5, 1, 3
D fossils, DNA

What you need to remember

evolved, millions, natural selection, survive, genes, fossils

10.3.2

A evolution
B Galapagos, Wallace, evaluated, published
C fossil record – organisms have changed over time (millions of years); finch beak and claws – birds best suited to available food survive and reproduce. Eventually all birds on the island have same characteristics; extinction – species that do not adapt to environmental changes die out; development of antibiotic-resistant bacteria – micro-organisms best suited for their environment survive and reproduce

What you need to remember

Darwin, evolve, selection, beaks, reproduce, peer, Wallace

10.3.3

A biodiversity, endangered, extinct
B ammonite, dinosaur
C outbreak of disease – whole population killed by a microorganism; prolonged drought – lack of water leads to death of whole population; introduction of new predators – whole population eaten before they have the chance to reproduce successfully; introduction of new competitors – lack of food / water causing death of whole population; deforestation – loss of food source or shelter leads to death of whole population
D many, high, many, shelter, survive, low, may not, die

What you need to remember

biodiversity, habitats, disease, extinct, endangered

10.3.4

A a species with only small numbers of organisms left in the world
B gene banks, captive breeding
C conservation – protecting a natural environment – increases an organisms chance of survival and reduces disruption to food chains; captive breeding – breeding animals in human-controlled environments – creates a healthy stable population that can be reintroduced back into the wild
D genetic, low, individuals

What you need to remember

endangered, conservation, captive, banks, survives

10.4.1

A DNA; chromosomes; genes
B gene – V; chromosome – U; cell – S; nucleus – T
C chromosomes, half, half, an egg, a sperm, fertilisation, 46

What you need to remember

nucleus, DNA, chromosomes, genes

10.4.2

A Maurice Wilkins, Rosalind Franklin
B two, helix, four, bases, identical twins
C characteristics, pea, nucleus, DNA, structure, helix, working, sharing, discoveries

What you need to remember

nucleus, two, helix, bases, Franklin, X-rays, Watson, helical / helix

10.4.3

A allele – different forms of the same gene; dominant allele – version of the gene always expressed if present; recessive allele – two copies are needed to be expressed in the organism
B freckles, freckles, no freckles
C all cells in Punnett square: Dd; all / 100% black fur
D

	D	d
D	DD	Dd
d	Dd	dd

75% black fur, 25% white fur

What you need to remember

alleles, dominant, recessive, Punnett

10.4.4

A genes, desired
B 1, 2
C 3, 1, 4, 2
D false, true, false, true

What you need to remember

characteristics, genes, foreign, cells

Big Idea 10 Pinchpoint

A this is an incorrect answer – 1 out of the 4 plants will have white flowers so a **1 in 4 or 1:3** likelihood
B this is an incorrect answer – ¾ of the plants will be **red-flowered** as they contain the dominant allele
C this is an incorrect answer – you have not combined the alleles Rr and Rr correctly
D this is the correct answer

Pinchpoint follow-up

A from top: 100%, 3:1, ½ (or 2/4), 1 in 4
B alleles, dominant, one copy, is, recessive, two copies, are
C a

	G	g
G	GG	Gg
g	Gg	gg

b 1 / 25% / 1 in 4 GG – red flowers
2 / 50% / 1 in 2 Gg – red flowers
1 / 25% / 1 in 4 gg – white flowers

D 25% (Punnett square should have 1 CC, 2Cc, and 1 cc)

Section 3 Revision questions

1 a caffeine / tobacco / ethanol (alcohol) [1]
  b paracetamol / antibiotic [1]
  c tobacco [1]
  d ethanol (alcohol) [1]
2 DNA [1], nucleus [1], chromosomes [1], genes [1], characteristic [1]
3 up and outwards [1], downwards [1], decreases [1], inwards [1]
4 a stomach – B [1]; gullet – A [1]; large intestine – D [1]
  b large molecules are broken down [1] into smaller molecules [1]

5   a   **two** from: carbohydrates [1], lipids [1], proteins [1], vitamins [1], minerals [1]
    b   e.g. heart disease / stroke / diabetes / some cancers [1]
    c   poor immune system / tired / lack of energy starvation / deficiency diseases [1]
6   a   glucose [1], oxygen [1]
    b   chloroplast [1]
    c   i   break down cell walls [1] so chlorophyll escapes / to decolourise the leaf [1]
        ii iodine turns from orange-yellow [1] to blue-black if starch is present [1]
    d   ethanol is flammable / can catch fire [1]
7   a   alveoli / alveolus [1]
    b   transfers gas between lungs and blood [1]; CO_2 out **and** O_2 in [1]
    c   large surface area [1] and thin wall / wall only one cell thick [1] to maximise rate of diffusion [1]
8   a   volume = difference between water levels / 4.0 – 0.5 [1] = 3.5 litres [1] [accept correct value for 2 marks without working]
    b   **two** from: exhaled air has: lower proportion of oxygen [1]; higher proportion of carbon dioxide [1]; higher proportion of water vapour [1]; is warmer [1] (or converse)
    c   e.g., asthma / smoking [1]
9   a   protein – to repair body tissues and make new cells; carbohydrates – main source of energy; lipids – to provide a store of energy, insulation and protect organs [2 for all correct, 1 for 1 correct]
    b   adds bulk to food [1] to keep it moving through intestine / help waste be pushed out of body / prevent constipation [1]
    c $\frac{2520}{8400} \times 100$ [1] = 30% [1]
    d   add Benedict's solution [1], heat (in water bath) [1]; if solution turns orange-red it contains sugar [1]
10 a   i   carbohydrase / amylase [1]
        ii breaks down carbohydrates / starch [1] into glucose / sugar molecules [1]
    b   speed up reactions [1] without being used up [1]
    c   live on fibre in the intestines [1]; make vitamins / vitamin K [1]
11 a   i   oxygen [1], water [1]   ii mitochondria [1]
    b   **two** from: anaerobic doesn't need oxygen, aerobic does [1]; anaerobic produces lactic acid, aerobic does not [1]; aerobic transfers more energy per glucose molecule [1]; aerobic produces carbon dioxide and water, anaerobic does not [1]
    c   i   fermentation (anaerobic respiration in yeast) [1]
        ii microorganism / yeast [1]
12 **six** from: organisms in prey species show variation [1]; those most adapted survive **and** reproduce [1]; named adaptation, e.g. fastest [1]; less well-adapted die [1]; genes from most-adapted individuals are passed onto next generation [1]; offspring are likely to display the advantageous characteristic / advantageous characteristic becomes more common [1]; reference to natural selection [1]; process repeated over many generations [1]; over time can lead to the development of a new species [1]
13 a   a dominant allele will always be expressed if is present [1]; two copies of a recessive allele are needed for it to be expressed in the organism [1]
    b
	Plant 1	
	P	p
Plant 2 P	Pp	pp
p	Pp	pp

[1]
Pp = purple, pp = white; ratio of Pp : pp is 1:1 [1] so 50% white / ½ white, or 1 white : 1 purple [1]
14 a   take genes from an organism that has a desired characteristic (foreign genes) [1]; place them into a plant or animal at a very early stage of development [1]; as the organism develops it will display the characteristics of the foreign genes [1]
    b   **two** from: disease- / pest-resistant plants [1] – higher yields / healthier plants / fewer chemicals used [1]; higher-yield plants [1] – more food produced / less land needed [1]; bacteria that produce medical drugs [1] – treat more people / produced quicker [1]; (other appropriate examples)
15 a   nicotine [1]
    b   1 200 000 [1]
    c   lung and throat cancer [1]
    d   **four** from: smoke contains chemicals that damage the cilia [1], which stops them moving mucus away from the lungs [1]; mucus traps microorganisms [1], so these are held within the lungs / airways [1], which could cause an infection [1]

Periodic table

key

| relative atomic mass |
| **atomic symbol** |
| name |
| atomic (proton) number |

Example: 1 **H** hydrogen 1

1	2											3	4	5	6	7	0
																	4 **He** helium 2
7 **Li** lithium 3	9 **Be** beryllium 4											11 **B** boron 5	12 **C** carbon 6	14 **N** nitrogen 7	16 **O** oxygen 8	19 **F** fluorine 9	20 **Ne** neon 10
23 **Na** sodium 11	24 **Mg** magnesium 12											27 **Al** aluminium 13	28 **Si** silicon 14	31 **P** phosphorus 15	32 **S** sulfur 16	35.5 **Cl** chlorine 17	40 **Ar** argon 18
39 **K** potassium 19	40 **Ca** calcium 20	45 **Sc** scandium 21	48 **Ti** titanium 22	51 **V** vanadium 23	52 **Cr** chromium 24	55 **Mn** manganese 25	56 **Fe** iron 26	59 **Co** cobalt 27	59 **Ni** nickel 28	63.5 **Cu** copper 29	65 **Zn** zinc 30	70 **Ga** gallium 31	73 **Ge** germanium 32	75 **As** arsenic 33	79 **Se** selenium 34	80 **Br** bromine 35	84 **Kr** krypton 36
85 **Rb** rubidium 37	88 **Sr** strontium 38	89 **Y** yttrium 39	91 **Zr** zirconium 40	93 **Nb** niobium 41	96 **Mo** molybdenum 42	[98] **Tc** technetium 43	101 **Ru** ruthenium 44	103 **Rh** rhodium 45	106 **Pd** palladium 46	108 **Ag** silver 47	112 **Cd** cadmium 48	115 **In** indium 49	119 **Sn** tin 50	122 **Sb** antimony 51	128 **Te** tellurium 52	127 **I** iodine 53	131 **Xe** xenon 54
133 **Cs** caesium 55	137 **Ba** barium 56	139 **La*** lanthanum 57	178 **Hf** hafnium 72	181 **Ta** tantalum 73	184 **W** tungsten 74	186 **Re** rhenium 75	190 **Os** osmium 76	192 **Ir** iridium 77	195 **Pt** platinum 78	197 **Au** gold 79	201 **Hg** mercury 80	204 **Tl** thallium 81	207 **Pb** lead 82	209 **Bi** bismuth 83	[209] **Po** polonium 84	[210] **At** astatine 85	[222] **Rn** radon 86
[223] **Fr** francium 87	[226] **Ra** radium 88	[227] **Ac*** actinium 89	[261] **Rf** rutherfordium 104	[262] **Db** dubnium 105	[266] **Sg** seaborgium 106	[264] **Bh** bohrium 107	[277] **Hs** hassium 108	[268] **Mt** meitnerium 109	[271] **Ds** darmstadtium 110	[272] **Rg** roentgenium 111	[285] **Cn** copernicium 112	[286] **Nh** nihonium 113	[289] **Fl** flerovium 114	[289] **Mc** moscovium 115	[293] **Lv** livermorium 116	[294] **Ts** tennessine 117	[294] **Og** oganesson 118

*The lanthanides (atomic numbers 58–71) and the actinides (atomic numbers 90–103) have been omitted.

OXFORD
UNIVERSITY PRESS

Great Clarendon Street, Oxford, OX2 6DP, United Kingdom

Oxford University Press is a department of the University of Oxford.
It furthers the University's objective of excellence in research,
scholarship, and education by publishing worldwide. Oxford is a
registered trade mark of Oxford University Press in the UK and in
certain other countries

© Oxford University Press 2018

The moral rights of the authors have been asserted

First published in 2018

All rights reserved. No part of this publication may be reproduced,
stored in a retrieval system, or transmitted, in any form or by any
means, without the prior permission in writing of Oxford University
Press, or as expressly permitted by law, by licence or under terms agreed
with the appropriate reprographics rights organization. Enquiries
concerning reproduction outside the scope of the above should be sent
to the Rights Department, Oxford University Press,
at the address above.

You must not circulate this work in any other form and you must
impose this same condition on any acquirer

British Library Cataloguing in Publication Data
Data available

978-0-19-842668-4

10 9 8 7 6 5 4 3 2

Paper used in the production of this book is a natural, recyclable
product made from wood grown in sustainable forests.
The manufacturing process conforms to the environmental regulations
of the country of origin.

Printed by CPI Group (UK) Ltd, Croydon CR0 4YY

Acknowledgements

The publisher and authors would like to thank the following for
permission to use photographs and other copyright material:

Cover image: Science Photo Library/Alamy Stock Photo; **p14**:
GIPhotoStock/Science Source; **p15**: PerWil/Shutterstock; **p18**: Sichon/
Shutterstock; **p28**: tlorna/Shutterstock; **p29**: Beautiful landscape/
Shutterstock; **p31(T)**: Petr Malyshev/Shutterstock; **p31(B)**: Iuliia
Syrotina/Shutterstock; **p32**: Dario Sabljak/Shutterstock.

All artwork by Aptara Inc., Q2A Media Services Ltd., and Phoenix
Photosetting

Every effort has been made to contact copyright holders of material
reproduced in this book. Any omissions will be rectified in subsequent
printings if notice is given to the publisher.